# EXOTIC CUISINE
# OF MAURITIUS

© EDITIONS DE L'OCEAN INDIEN (2006)

Photos © : **Christian Bossu-Picat**
Page layout : **Christian Bossu-Picat and Pascal Lagesse**
Prepress : **Précigraph Ltd, Mauritius**
Reprint : **Ajanta Offset & Packagings Ltd., India (2013)**

Published by
**EDITIONS DE L'OCEAN INDIEN**
Stanley, Rose-Hill
Mauritius
Tel. : (230) 464 6761
Fax : (230) 464 3445
www.eoi-info.com

ISBN : 978-99903-0-542-5

PHILIPPE LENOIR
RAYMOND DE RAVEL
JEAN-PIERRE LENOIR

# EXOTIC CUISINE
# OF MAURITIUS

PHOTOS BY
CHRISTIAN BOSSU-PICAT

EDITIONS DE L'OCEAN INDIEN

# OUR FATHERS' CUISINE

IT CAN BE AFRICAN, CHINESE, INDIAN, PAKISTANI OR FRENCH AND EVEN A MIXTURE OF ALL THESE ... A PERFECT REFLECTION OF THE MAURITIAN POPULATION: MULTICOLOURED. THE CONTRASTING PATTERN OF COLOURS CAN BE FOUND ON OUR PLATES THROUGH A MAGICAL VERSE. THE MAURITIAN CUISINE HAS THE ABILITY TO REFLECT WHO WE ARE IN REAL LIFE. SCENTS AND TASTES IMPORTED FROM THE ORIENT AND OCCIDENT. A FLORILEGIUM, BUT ALSO A CHARM WHICH BRINGS AN ETERNAL REBIRTH TO THE ART OF COOKING. THE BOOK REVEALS THE TALENT OF MEN WHO DEDICATED THEIR LIVES INVENTING, BALANCING AND COOKING.

"EXOTIC CUISINE OF MAURITIUS" WAS INSPIRED BY THE AMALGAMATION OF THIS MAGICAL CUISINE WHICH EMERGED ON AN ORDINARY DAY WHEN A RECIPE WAS INVENTED OR IMPROVED AS A CONSEQUENCE OF THE "GENIUS" AND ALSO THE SPONTANEOUS CREATIVITY OF THOSE WHO WERE COOKING ON THAT DAY. THIS BOOK IS NOT ONLY THE RESULT OF A ONE-DAY FANTASY, BUT ALSO OF A CONTINUOUS THINKING PROCESS EXPERIMENTING WITH WHAT NATURE HAS GENEROUSLY GIVEN US. CITING THE POET, MY FATHER PHILIPPE WROTE ON THE PREFACE OF THE FIRST EDITION OF THIS BOOK THAT; " THE MAURITIAN CUISINE HAS ESCAPED THE BOREDOM WHICH WAS BORN FROM UNIFORMITY."

TO THIS I CAN TESTIFY. I HAD THE CHANCE TO GROW UP IN A FAMILY WHICH LOVES FOOD. MY CHILDHOOD AND TEENAGE YEARS WERE NOURISHED BY EPIC GASTRONOMIC DISCUSSIONS PRAISING WITH VEHEMENCE AND PASSION THE MERITS OF A CERTAIN MEAT OR OF A SPECIFIC RECIPE, VISITS TO FAMOUS RESTAURANTS OR SMALL, SIMPLE BISTROS AND THE PLEASANT READING OF THE LIFE OF LEGENDARY MASTERS OF GASTRONOMY. THE KITCHEN WAS THE MOST IMPORTANT AREA OF THE HOUSE ...

The idea of this book was born from a passion. The want of tasting good food resulted in the need of encouraging other people to eat good food. Philippe Lenoir and Raymond de Ravel regrouped and encouraged those who had culinary secrets and the generosity to share them. All this was done with simplicity as life is complicated enough and we cannot forget to taste the simple pleasures of the table.

Philippe Lenoir and Raymond de Ravel are no longer there to read this new edition of "Exotic cuisine of Mauritius". This book is also to pay a tribute to these talented men and a way of sharing those gifts with you. As a conclusion, we quote a few comments of the authors.

"The cook, as the poet, is often tempted by inspiration ... without the certitude that the Muse will be a masterpiece. Always dare from what we have created and avoid following our recipes as a medical prescription where milligrams are balanced ..."

JEAN-PIERRE LENOIR

# ISLAND OF ALL PLEASURES

WHAT ELSE TO SAY ABOUT AN ISLAND, EXCEPT THAT IT IS SURROUNDED BY WATER !

I NEED TO PRECISE THAT IT IS BEAUTIFUL, ACTUALLY AMAZINGLY BEAUTIFUL... IT IS NOT RESPONSIBLE FOR ANYTHING AS NATURE CREATED IT AS SUCH. WHAT A CRAZY IDEA DID IT HAVE ONE DAY TO SUDDENLY APPEAR IN THE MIDDLE OF THE OCEAN AS A SPARKLING JEWEL IN A CASE. A WHIM OF NATURE WHICH DOES THINGS RIGHT...! THE RESULT OF THIS DIVINE WISH IS TO OFFER TO THE INDIAN OCEAN, ONE OF ITS MOST BEAUTIFUL ISLANDS. THIS WAS GODS' DECISION. SOMETIMES NONCHALANTLY FLOATING IN A CALM SUMMER OCEAN, AT OTHER TIMES FRAGILE AND BATTERED IN THE

WINTER WIND, IT STAYS, ALL YEAR ROUND, THIS MAGICAL ISLAND WHERE THE SMILE NEVER FADES. ITS ETHNIC AND CULTURAL DIVERSITY, BUT ALSO THE GENEROSITY OF THE INHABITANTS FORM A MAGICAL COMPLEXITY.

# Mauritian gastronomy

Mauritian gastronomy evolved over a period of two and a half centuries. Our créole cuisine grew from a modest start with the first French settlers and the help of African, Malagasy, and Indian labour. Regional recipes of "Vieille France" were adapted to the new environment, utilizing tropical products and Oriental spices brought by travellers. The massive immigration of the Indians, followed by that of the Chinese, contributed an exotic  touch to French cookery as these cuisines became entrenched in the colony. The boredom spawned from standardization never remotely threatened Mauritian cuisine; it is noteworthy that dear Albion never influenced, or made a mark on its style! A remarkable feat indeed ...

While some of the recipes in this book have been signed by the authors and by other gastronomes invited to lend their contribution, most are current fare deserving the traditional anonymity of regional cookery. Some recipes have been culled from old family notebooks dating from the past century or from the pre-war years - a time gone by when colloquial barter reigned supreme: "three cents of **saffran**" was exactly enough for one dish - one cent represented a base measure: one bought one cent of chillies or five cents of coal. A chicken for a curry, or a fricassée, was simply fifty cents of chicken, and "une moque de riz" (one quarter pound) was enough to feed one person. It is interesting to note that, in times when cholesterol was not a known threat, people exclusively cooked with pure pork lard, except for the poor who used cheap coconut oil.

Even if the fifty cent chicken of yore has given way to the fifty rupee roaster, a great number of Mauritians do their very best to stay faithful to the traditions of the past and to maintain its impeccable standards.

We would like to point out to our foreign readers that we wrote this book with several objectives in mind. We hoped that a good many recipes might be recreated elsewhere without too much difficulty, since many tropical foods are now available worldwide. Those recipes listing indigenous island ingredients, and for which there are no substitutes, are to be savoured vicariously! Our visitors are therefore advised to store their gustatory memories preciously ... We confess to having done our best to lure those who are still strangers to our shores. We would love to seduce them, as we have other vacationers, with our exotic flavours and sleepy lagoons, our scintillating Capricorn galaxies and our séga dancers who Marcel Cabon, the writer and poet, described as having bodies more supple than fire ...

**Bon appetit**! And **bon voyage** en route towards the Star and Key of the Indian Ocean, to the Isle of Paul and Virginie, to the island of the dodo - this infamous bird which, it is rumoured, the Dutch tried in vain to incorporate into the kingdom of gastronomy ...

**Philippe LENOIR**

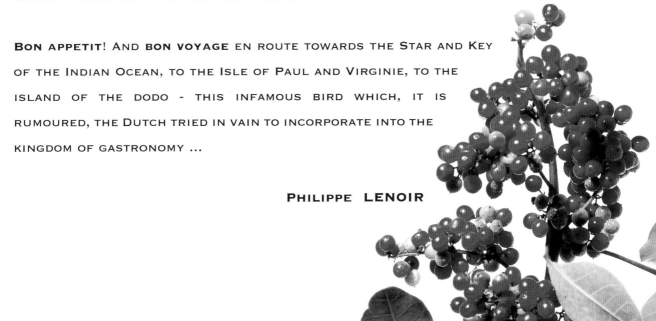

*Red pepper*

# TRADITIONAL AND PICTURESQUE MAURITIAN KITCHEN UTENSILS

**THE CURRY STONE** : SQUARE OR RECTANGULAR SLAB OF STONE MEASURING APPROXIMATELY 12 TO 18 INCHES AND PAIRED WITH A BABA - CYLINDRICAL PIECE OF STONE IN THE FORM OF A ROLLING PIN, USED TO CRUSH THE SPICES FOR A MASSALA AND SOME OTHER PREPARATIONS.

**MORTAR AND PESTLE** : STONE 6 TO 8 INCHES ACROSS, SCOOPED TO FORM A DEEP WELL INTO WHICH A STONE PESTLE FITS LIKE A GLOVE. USED FOR CRUSHING CHILLIES, GARLIC, GINGER AND VARIOUS OTHER SPICES. SMALL WOODEN MORTARS ARE NOW MORE FREQUENTLY USED FOR THIS PURPOSE.

COFFEE WAS GROUND IN A MORTAR FASHIONED FROM THE TRUNK OF A TREE, WITH A WOODEN PESTLE. BOTH WERE BUFFED AND POLISHED BEFORE USAGE.

**WOK OR CHINESE "CARAILLE"** : LARGE CIRCULAR ROUNDED PAN MADE OF WROUGHT IRON OR OTHER METAL. IDEAL FOR THE FAST MIXING OF INGREDIENTS (STIR FRYING) AND RAPID COOKING. THE WOK HAS THE ADVANTAGE OF EVEN HEAT DISTRIBUTION AND LARGE SURFACE EVAPORATION IDEAL FOR THE REDUCTION OF SAUCES. THE WOK CAN BE USED SUCCESSFULLY TO COOK DISHES OTHER THAN CHINESE!

**DEKTI** : LIGHT ALUMINIUM DISH WITH A TIGHT FITTING COVER (MAY BUCKLE EASILY - THEREFORE, CHOOSE THE HEAVIER ONES). VERY CONVENIENT, PARTICULARLY TO CARRY FOODS. COMES IN A GREAT SELECTION OF SIZES.

**RAPE (PRONOUNCED "RAP"):** GRATER MADE OF TIN WITH DIFFERENT HOLE SIZES WHICH HAS SURVIVED INTACT AND IS PREFERRED TO ELECTRIC GRATERS IN MANY HOMES. IT IS MANUFACTURED LOCALLY.

**CARAILLE :** DEEP CIRCULAR COOKING PAN MADE OF CAST IRON. USED REGULARLY FOR FRYING. THE OLDEST CARAILLES, SEASONED BY THE MEMORY OF COUNTLESS DISHES, ARE WONT TO MAKE THE BEST MEALS - OR SO GOES AN OLD PROVERB!

**BILLOT :** HEAVY WOOD CHOPPING BLOCK WHICH OCCUPIES A PLACE OF HONOUR IN MANY KITCHENS. ALL THE MORE REVERED FOR THE VETERAN SCARS AND GOUGES IT BEARS. A GOOD SCRUBBING IS ADVISED AFTER EACH USE.

**VAN (PRONOUNCED "VANN"):** CIRCULAR FLAT WICKER TRAY WITH A RAISED EDGE. MADE OUT OF ALOE OR VACOAS FIBRES, MEASURING 16 TO 20 INCHES. USED TO SIFT OUT, WITH A FEW TWISTS OF THE WRIST, ANY DUST AND DEBRIS FROM RICE AND LENTILS.

**TAWA :** A GRIDDLE MADE OF CAST-IRON - THE IDEAL UTENSIL FOR COOKING "FARATHAS", "CHAPPATTI" ETC. .. CAN BE USED ON ELECTRIC OR GAS RANGES, AND ALSO ON A COAL OR WOOD FIRE.

**JAMA :** LARGE PERFORATED SPOON USED IN THE PREPARATION OF SPECIAL FRIED FOODS SUCH AS THE "BOONDEE" AND "BADIAH" - SMALL CAKES MADE WITH CHICK-PEA FLOUR.

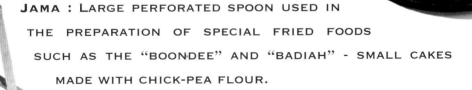

# GETTING TO KNOW AND APPRECIATE ...
## SPICES & HERBS

*IT MIGHT PROVE REWARDING FOR THE VISITOR TO ACQUAINT HIMSELF WITH THE NAMES AND DESCRIPTIONS OF THE MOST COMMONLY USED SPICES AND HERBS IN OUR CUISINE. WE HAVE ADDED SOME PERSONAL COMMENTS WHEREVER APPROPRIATE. BASIC SPICES AND HERBS, COMMON TO MOST CUISINES AND USED ALMOST UNIVERSALLY: GARLIC - BLACK AND GREEN PEPPER - THYME - PARSLEY - NUTMEG - CLOVES.*

**CHILLIES (PIMENTS) :** USED FRESH, DRIED, OR RIPE (RED). NOT COUNTING THE BELL PEPPER ("GROS PIMENT" IN MAURITIAN), THERE ARE SEVERAL TYPES WITH DIFFERENT FLAVOURS, DEGREES OF HEAT, SHAPES AND SIZES. THE TINIEST IS TO BE FEARED THE MOST: THE SAVVY CREOLE EXPRESSION "ENE TI PIMENT" (MEANING LITTLE DEVIL) HITS THE NAIL ON THE HEAD WHEN REFERRING TO SOMEONE OF ORNERY TEMPERAMENT. TO NAME A FEW: PIMENT **CABRI**, PIMENT **CURRY** (USED SPECIFICALLY FOR THAT DISH), PIMENT **CIPAYE**, PIMENT **MARTIN**. CHILLIES SHOULD BE USED PARSIMONIOUSLY - IN GOOD CUISINE THEY ENHANCE, AND DO NOT OVERPOWER PRIMARY FLAVOURS.

*DRIED CHILLI*

**GINGER (GINGEMBRE) :** ROOT WITH VERY THIN SKIN WHICH IS EASILY SCRAPED OFF. USUALLY USED AFTER BEING CRUSHED IN A MORTAR. MERGES HAPPILY WITH GARLIC. IS ALSO AVAILABLE IN POWDERED FORM.

*GINGER*

**MASSALA :** COTOMILI (CORIANDER) SEEDS FROM A SMALL PLANT, THE LEAVES OF WHICH ARE ALSO KNOWN AS CHINESE PARSLEY. USED EXTENSIVELY IN INDIAN COOKERY. THE DRIED SEEDS ARE CRUSHED AND USED IN CURRY POWDER. MASSALA PASTE, THE BASE OF SOME CURRIES, IS MADE UP IN LARGE PART OF THOSE SEEDS.

**CURRY POWDER :** BLEND OF POWDERED TURMERIC, (SAFFRON OF THE INDIES), CORIANDER SEEDS, PEPPER, GINGER, CLOVES, CINNAMON, CUMIN, ANISE, AND CHILLIES. OTHER SPICES CAN BE ADDED TO THE MIXTURE. CAN BE PREPARED FROM SCRATCH OR BOUGHT READY-MADE, WITH OR WITHOUT CHILLIES.

**CURRY LEAVES (CARRIPOULE):** SPELLING VARIES FROM PLACE TO PLACE - CARRIPILLAY OR KALOUPILE IN RÉUNION). MEDIUM SIZE

*CURRY LEAVES*

BUSH WITH SMALL AROMATIC LEAVES WHICH CAN BE USED, NOT ONLY IN CURRIES, BUT ALSO IN FRICASSÉES AND OTHER DISHES TO WHICH IT LENDS A HAUNTINGLY PLEASANT FLAVOUR.

**QUATRE EPICES (ALL SPICE)** : PLANT WITH AROMATIC LEAVES HAVING THE FLAVOUR OF FOUR DIFFERENT SPICES: CINNAMON, CLOVES, NUTMEG, AND PEPPER. ITS USE IS SIMILAR TO THAT OF CURRY LEAVES. ITS SEED IS ALSO KNOWN AS THE JAMAICA PEPPER.

**TAMARIN – TAMARIND** : FRUIT OF THE TAMARIND TREE, THE ACID FLAVOURED PULP OF WHICH IS MADE INTO A PASTE AND FASHIONED INTO BALLS. UTILIZED IN CERTAIN DISHES, NOTABLY CURRIES.

**COTOMILI - CORIANDER** (SEE MASSALA ABOVE) : BOTH THE LEAVES AND SEEDS ARE USED.

**COMBAVA** : SMALL CITRUS WITH HIGHLY PERFUMED SKIN WHICH IS ADDED TO SOME CHUTNEYS. RARELY USED IN MAURITIUS WHERE IT IS SCARCE, BUT VERY POPULAR IN REUNION. NOT A SPICE.

CORIANDER

**VARGON** : POWDER MADE FROM A MIXTURE OF SPICES, REMINISCENT OF CURRY, BUT INCLUDING FRESH TURMERIC ROOT (SAFFRAN VERT) AND ONION, IT IS PREPARED FOR IMMEDIATE USE, BUT CAN ALSO BE BOUGHT IN DRIED BALLS. USED TO MAKE CURRY.

**CARDAMOM (CARDAMOME – LAITI OR ILAITI)** : SEEDS FROM PODS OF A SMALL TREE INDIGENOUS TO INDIA. THE LORE OF AGES HAS ALWAYS RELISHED ATTRIBUTING CERTAIN MAGICAL PROPERTIES TO SPICES ... CARDAMOM IS NOT EXEMPT... AND AMONG OTHER VIRTUES IT IS REPUTED TO BE AN APHRODISIAC AND TO COMBAT THE OFFENSIVE TELL-TALE ODOUR OF GARLIC.

IT IS FREQUENTLY USED IN ORIENTAL COOKERY AND IS AN INTEGRAL COMPONENT OF CURRY POWDERS.

NOTE THAT MANY SPICES, WHEN NOT AVAILABLE FRESH, CAN BE BOUGHT, (USUALLY GROUND INTO A POWDER), IN SMALL PACKETS FROM THE SHELVES OF GROCERY STORES.

ALL SPICE

FENNEL SEEDS    CLOVES

MUSTARD    NUTMEG

# STARTERS

# TROPICAL FRITTERS

*The long, slender, firm textured variety of eggplant, turns into wonderful crunchy pre-dinner snacks or appetizers. Fritters made from the large globe-shaped eggplant are one of the satellite dishes served with rice. They are best when sprinkled lightly with lemon juice with some chillies and pepper added. The same for the long and thick chillies called "Piment Cari"*

# CHILLI (OR EGGPLANT) FRITTERS

## INGREDIENTS

25 to 30 long "Curry" chillies, with stems intact, or three large globe-shaped eggplants
Oil for frying

## FRITTER BATTER :

2 cups flour, sifted

1 egg yolk

2 cups water

2 tablespoons oil

Pinch of pepper and turmeric

Thyme and parsley

1 teaspoon salt

1 egg white, whipped (optional)

In a bowl mix together the flour, egg yolk and water. Stir in the oil and spices, mixing well until the batter is smooth and free of lumps. For a lighter batter, fold in the whipped egg white just before using.

Dip the chillies or eggplants in batter and fry in very hot oil for 2 to 3 minutes until they turn golden brown. Drain well and serve immediately.

---

GHADIAK (GADJACK): SPELLED MISCELLANEOUSLY. EQUIVALENT TO COCKTAIL SNACKS - SERVED WITH APERITIFS PRECEDING A MEAL. THE BEST ARE THOSE SOLD AT STREET CORNERS OR IN MARKETS - THE MOST POPULAR IS PROBABLY THE GATEAU PIMENT, A FRITTER MADE WITH CRUSHED DHOLL AND CHILLIES.

---

SAMOUSSA: DEEP-FRIED PASTRY IN THE SHAPE OF A TRIANGLE WHICH IS FILLED WITH A SPICED VEGETABLE OR MEAT FILLING. IT IS BEST WHEN CONSUMED FRESHLY PREPARED AND HOT.

# PATTYPAN STUFFED WITH CRAB

## INGREDIENTS (4 SERVINGS)

8 young pattypan

250 gms crab meat

1 boiled egg

3 tomatoes

1 onion

Garlic and parsley

2 tablespoons mayonnaise

Boil the pattypan for 30 minutes. Make a large hole on the top of the pattypan.

Sauté the crab meat with the minced onion, the garlic, parsley and chopped tomatoes. Add the crushed egg and the mayonnaise. Mix well and stuff the pattypan. Serve cold.

JEAN-PIERRE LENOIR

# SALAD OF HEART PALM

## INGREDIENTS : 4 TO 5 SERVINGS

1 fresh heart of palm, sliced thinly

## VINAIGRETTE:

4 tablespoons olive oil
1 tablespoon vinegar
Salt and pepper

Prepare the heart of palm but without cooking it... Use only the most tender part of the heart, reserving the rest to make achards. Use a sharp knife, preferably stainless steel, to cut it into very thin slices.

It is crucial here to keep the flesh white. In order to prevent oxidation – which can happen alarmingly fast, take special precautions :

... keep the heart well submerged in the water/milk liquid (to which you may add a little salt) while peeling and cutting, and until almost ready to serve.

... Drain well, but rapidly.

... Add the vinaigrette just before serving.

## NOTE:

*Use salt and pepper sparingly, for the delicate flavour of the heart of palm bears no interference. Onion, and garlic, are anathema to the purist; naturally, this is merely a question of taste... The salad should be delightfully crunchy; therefore, toss in the vinaigrette at the very last moment.*

*Heart of palm...*
*... comes encased in a multitude of protective fibrous sheaths. A certain amount of skill and strength is required to retrieve its edible delicate core. Then, utmost care must be taken to protect its ivory white flesh from changing colour through oxidation.*

# Salad of octopus and heart of palm

## Ingredients : 5 to 6 servings

1 heart of palm – medium sized, very fresh, and prepared as for the salad of heart of palm, raw and cut in thin slices, submerged in a water and milk bath.

$1^1/2$ lbs octopus – boiled for one hour in a pressure cooker, using plenty of water to keep it from sticking.

Discard the viscous membranes and suction cups, and cut into fine juliennes.

## Vinaigrette :

4 tablespoons olive oil

2 tablespoons vinegar or more as desired

$1/2$ cup sherry

4 small white onions, finely sliced

4 tablespoons shallots, finely minced

4 tablespoons chopped parsley

6 hard boiled eggs, mashed

dash of mustard, salt and pepper to taste

In a salad bowl mix the ingredients for the vinaigrette.  Add the octopus and heart of palm (drained and pressed dry in cloth).  Stir well and serve.

RAYMOND DE RAVEL

# BOUILLON OF TECS-TECS

## INGREDIENTS : 6 TO 8 SERVINGS

1 1/2 lbs tecs-tecs

2 tablespoons oil

1 small onion

2 teaspoons crushed garlic

1/2 teaspoon turmeric

3 curry leaves

2 long chillies

thyme, parsley, salt and pepper

1/4 lb ripe tomatoes (pommes d'amour), crushed

Wash tecs-tecs in several changes of water to rid them of sand. Cover with water and boil for five minutes. Strain, reserving the broth, and discard the shells after picking out the nail-sized mollusc.

Heat the oil in a saucepan. Add the onion, garlic, and turmeric and cook gently until onion is golden. Add the curry leaves, chillies, thyme, and parsley and cook for one minute. Stir in the tomatoes, and cook until sauce is reduced. Stir in the tec-tec meat and the reserved broth. Season with salt and pepper, and cook for about five minutes.

Serve with rice and your favourite chutney.

If you prefer to serve the tec-tec bouillon as a soup, add water to the dish without diluting it too much, and serve with fried croutons. Garnish with a slice of lemon or tomato if desired.

## NOTE :

*The tec-tec, in spite of its name, is not related to the* **maman tec-tec***, another small, crab-like crustacean, which is found burried in the sand, and is equally sought after!*

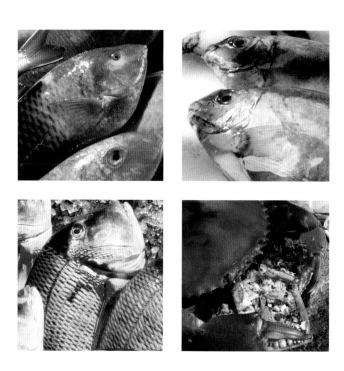

# FISH, SEAFOOD

# BOUILLABAISSE CRÉOLE

## INGREDIENTS : 7 TO 8 SERVINGS

1 white firm-fleshed fish weighing 4 to 5 lbs or 3 lbs fish fillets
3 lbs small fish — rougets, vieilles, cateaux, etc ..
3 lbs small crabs
3 to 4 lobsters, $1^1/4$ to $1^1/2$ (half a lobster per person)
2 lbs bigorneaux and/or 1 lb tecs-tecs
1 lb fresh or frozen shrimps (with heads)
4 tablespoons olive oil
$1/2$ lb onions, sliced
1 lb ripe tomatoes or pommes d'amour, crushed
1 teaspoon dried turmeric or 1 gram spanish saffron smoked in one cup boiling water
$1^1/2$ tablespoons crushed garlic or 10 cloves, minced
2 teaspoons crushed ginger root
6 long curry chillies
8 curry leaves
1 bouquet thyme and parsley
$1/4$ lb shallots or chives, minced
4 cups water
$1/2$ bottle dry white wine
4 bell peppers, seeded and chopped
$1/2$ lb sandwich bread (pain de mie)
3 lemons
Salt, whole and ground pepper

Select a prime quality fish (capitaine, gueule pavée, vacoas, etc ... ) Carve the fillet off the fish, fry them on both sides until well browned, and reserve. Fry the fish head briefly, and reserve.

Fry the small fishes quickly in very hot oil. Crush them with two cups boiling water, strain, and reserve broth. Wash the crabs well. Reserve a few of the larger ones. Fry the others briefly, crush with 2 cups boiling water, strain, and reserve broth.

Plunge the lobsters in boiling water for one minute. Cut them in half lengthwise, head included, and reserve. Boil bigorneaux and/or tecs-tecs in two cups water for 10 minutes. Strain the broth, and reserve. Pick the meat out of the shells, and reserve.

Fry the shrimps in very hot oil one minute, or until they turn pink.

In a large kettle, heat olive oil. Add onions and sauté until wilted. Add tomatoes, garlic, ginger, saffron, herbs, chillies, and curry leaves. Cook over high heat for 3 to 4 minutes. Stir in all of the reserved broths, the crabs, bigorneaux and tecs-tecs meat, and the fish head. Bring to a boil and cook over high heat for 10 minutes. Add the white wine, shrimps, whole reserved crabs, shallots or chives, and bell peppers. Cover and simmer for 10 minutes. Add the lobster halves and simmer for 15 minutes. Add the fried fillets to the soup a few minutes before serving .

Serve with fried croutons and a garlicky rouille or spicy lemon sauce. Creole tradition dictates that a great dish of rice be on the table with a satellite assortment of chutneys and mazavaroos.

**PHILIPPE LENOIR**

# Silver bream with creme fraiche

## Ingredients : 6 to 8 servings

1 Silver Bream – gueule pavée– weighing about 4 lbs or use a first choice firm, white-fleshed fish such as capitaine, sacrechien, vacoas, etc ...

10 tablespoons butter

1 onion, thinly sliced

1 teaspoon crushed garlic

1 teaspoon crushed ginger

1/2 cup dry white wine

1 teaspoon leaf thyme

1 teaspoon chopped parsley

1 1/4 cups crème fraîche

1/2 lb chopped mushrooms, fresh or canned

Salt and pepper


Fillet the fish, retaining skin, and cut into 6 to 8 portions. Save the head and bones to make fish stock.

Place butter to heat in a saucepan large enough to hold the pieces of fish side by side. Add onions, garlic, and ginger, and cook gently for 2 to 3 minutes. Add fish, skin down, and cook for 5 minutes. Add the wine and herbs, sprinkle lightly with salt and pepper, and cook over gentle heat for 30 minutes. Transfer fish to another dish and reserve while you make the sauce. Make sure that the wine has reduced completely. Add crème fraîche and mushrooms to the pan and mix well. Place fish back into sauce, and simmer gently for about 10 minutes.

Serve with rice or potatoes.

JEAN-PIERRE LENOIR

# SWEET AND SOUR FISH WITH GINGER

### INGREDIENTS

1 1/2 lbs fresh fish
1 oz vermicelli or rice noodles
Oil for frying
1/4 lb fresh ginger root
1 carrot
1 red bell pepper
10 tablespoons water
5 tablespoons vinegar
2 cloves garlic, minced
2 tablespoons sugar
1/2 teaspoon salt
1 tablespoon cornflour (maizena)
2 tablespoons oil
1/4 lb bean sprouts

Select a white firm-fleshed fish. Fry the fish until brown and crisp on both sides. Remove from pan and place to drain on paper towels. Keep warm. Fry the noodles in hot oil until puffed and golden. Remove and reserve.

Peel ginger and cut into very thin slices. Cut carrot in slender sticks. Seed bell pepper and cut into thin slices. In a bowl, mix together water, vinegar, garlic, sugar, salt, and cornflour.

Heat oil in a skillet. Add the ginger, carrot sticks, bell pepper slices, and bean sprouts. Cook briefly over high heat. Add in the water and vinegar mixture, and cook, stirring, for two minutes or until sauce thickens.

Place fish on a platter and surround it with lettuce leaves. Pour the hot sauce evenly over the fish and top with the reserved fried noodles. Serve immediately.

**(LA PAGODE RESTAURANT, GRAND BAIE)**

# CHARCOAL GRILLED RED SNAPPER

### INGREDIENTS : 5 TO 6 SERVINGS

1 Red Snapper (Sacréchien) weighing approx. 4 lbs

1 small white onion

2 cloves garlic

1 bouquet thyme and parsley

4 tablespoons butter or margarine

1 lemon

1 tomato

1 bell pepper

Salt and pepper

Have the fish scaled and cleaned, and rinse it well. Season the interior of the fish with salt and pepper and stuff it with the following mixture: chopped onion, garlic, parsley, thyme, 2 tablespoons of butter, a few slices of seeded tomato and bell pepper. Sprinkle with the juice of half the lemon.

Spread the rest of the butter evenly over the sides of the fish. Season lightly with salt and pepper, and arrange a few slices of tomato and bell pepper over both surfaces of the fish.

Place the fish over a large banana leaf. Sprinkle with the rest of the lemon juice and wrap the fish securely in the leaf so that it is almost completely sealed in.

Place the fish on a rack 12 inches above a red hot charcoal barbecue fire. Cook for 15 to 20 minutes on each side, turning the fish over very carefully.

NOTE : *If a barbecue is not available, the fish can be baked or grilled in an oven (45 to 50 minutes at 375 to 400°).*

*When the fish is done, unfold the leaf and slide it onto a platter. Sprinkle with more lemon juice, and garnish with sliced tomatoes, parsley, lemon wedges etc ... If banana leaves are not available one can use aluminium foil which is in fact more practical for the cooking but... less exotic.*

*Other types of fish suitable for this recipe are the "Grosses vieilles", the very delicate "Vieille La Boue" (types of rock cod), the vivanneau (snapper), etc... For firmer-fleshed fish such as capitaine, barois, vacoas (types of scavenger), allow about 10 more minutes of cooking time.*

**PIPO LENOIR**

# BRAISED CAPITAINE
# WITH GREEN PEPPERCORNS

### INGREDIENTS : 6 TO 8 SERVINGS

1 capitaine weighing about 4 lbs

(or use a top quality, firm, white-fleshed fish such as vacoas, sacréchien etc ...

or use 3 lbs thick fish fillets of your choice)

5 tablespoons oil

$1/2$ lb large white onions, cut in thick slices

$1/4$ lb ripe tomatoes or pommes d'amour, chopped

1 teaspoon, each, crushed garlic and ginger

1 tablespoon chopped parsley

2 teaspoons thyme leaves

6 curry leaves or a bouquet of herbs

$1/4$ lb carrots, sliced

2 bell peppers, seeded and sliced

$1^1/2$ cups water

2 tablespoons green peppercorns

$1/2$ cup dry white wine or $1/4$ cup dry vermouth

1 tablespoon lightly salted butter

Salt and pepper

1 lemon

Fillet the fish, and cut into 12 pieces.

Heat the oil in a casserole, and sauté onions for one or two minutes. Add the tomatoes, garlic, ginger and herbs, and cook for about 10 minutes, or until sauce is thick and rich. Add the fillets, placing them over the onions, so that fish will not stick to the pan while braising. Add the carrots, bell peppers, and water. Spoon the green peppercorns, and the wine or vermouth evenly over the fish. Cover and cook over low heat for 30 minutes. Season with salt and pepper, cover, and simmer gently for 15 more minutes.

Transfer the fish to a pre-heated platter, spoon the sauce on top, and decorate each piece of fillet with a thin slice of lemon.

PHILIPPE LENOIR

# FISH CURRY

## INGREDIENTS : 5 TO 6 SERVINGS

1 fish, weighing about 4 lbs, filleted, or 3 lbs fish fillets

Use the traditional curry sauce or sauce made with packets of curry powder for fish, with or without chillies.

A great number of fish may be used to make curry. We shall list a few of the Island species suitable to make curry: Capitaine, Vacoas, Gueule pavée, Sacréchien, Carangue, Thon, Mulet etc ... These are all firm-fleshed fish — it is best to avoid fish whose flesh is too fine to hold its shape when cooked. Cateaux and Vieilles are therefore not recommended. The Cordonnier is among the tastiest fish for curry and can be used whole or filleted. A note of caution: cordonniers have a reputation for causing indigestion when eaten at night!

Fry the fish (whole, cut in slices, or filleted) until brown and cooked through. Add to the curry sauce and simmer for 10 minutes.

Accompany the curry with basmati rice, a dish of brèdes, and a choice of chutneys - a popular choice for lunch at the beach when sun, sea, and sand have sharpened appetites!

## A GOOD CURRY SAUCE

### INGREDIENTS
4 tablespoons veg oil
2 onions
3 very ripe pommes d'amour
2 table spoons curry powder
Thyme, parsley, garlic and crushed ginger

Brown the chopped onions in hot oil. Add crushed or chopped pommes d'amour. Cook for five minutes. Stir in the curry powder dissolved in one cup of hot water, thyme, parsley, garlic and ginger. Simmer for 15 minutes and season with salt and pepper. This sauce is perfect for all sorts of curries.

**CURRY** (CARRI - KHURDI): THOUGHT TO HAVE ORIGINATED IN PERSIA, CURRY WAS OUR GIFT "PAR EXCELLENCE" FROM INDIA. THE POPULAR MADRAS CURRY POWDER IS PARTICULARLY HIGHLY SPICED. TOMATOES ARE EXCLUDED IN CURRIES IN INDIA, WHEREAS IN MAURITIUS THE DARLING POMME D'AMOUR INSINUATES ITSELF IN PRACTICALLY EVERY CURRIED DISH! (EXCEPT THE DRY CURRY)

# VINDAYE OF OCTOPUS

## INGREDIENTS : 7 TO 8 SERVINGS

1 octopus weighing 3 to 4 lbs
5 to 6 tablespoons oil
1 tablespoon powdered turmeric
2 tablespoons vinegar
4 cloves garlic, crushed
1 teaspoon crushed ginger
$^1/_4$ lb pearl onions, peeled
4 or more long chillies, split lengthwise
Thyme, chopped parsley, salt, and pepper

Wash the octopus thoroughly, prefer avoiding the proverbial "beating"! (the octopus is pounded on the currystone with the baba also made of stone to tender the flesh). Add one cup of water to the cooker and set timer for 30 minutes.

Let cool and remove from the cooker. Do not discard the suction cups still attached to the tentacles and make certain that the octopus is tender – otherwise put it back in the cooker for a few more minutes. Cut the tentacles and the head into one inch pieces.

Heat the oil. Stir the turmeric in the vinegar and add to the pan with the garlic and ginger. Sauté briefly and then add the pieces of octopus, the pearl onions, chillies, thyme, parsley, salt and pepper. Stir gently for two to three minutes over medium heat. Remove from heat, cool to warm, and transfer to a deep dish.

*NOTE : This recipe is a "dry" version of the classic vindaye preparation. It utilizes powdered turmeric rather than the fresh root and is more digestible since little oil is used. The classic vindaye with its liberal use of oil will keep almost indefinitely, whereas the dry vindaye will keep for only 6 to 7 days in the refrigerator. This simple and excellent recipe can also be adapted for fish and meats.*
*It is interesting to note that achards can be treated similarly – the dry version being more perishable but healthier than the other which relies heavily on oil for its longevity.*

**PHILIPPE LENOIR**

VINDYE (VINDAYE): ORIGINATED IN PORTUGAL - VIGNA (WINE), ALHO (GARLIC), EQUALS GARLIC WINE ... MOST LIKELY THIS WAS WINE TURNED-TO-VINEGAR - TO WHICH GARLIC WAS ADDED- AND USED FOR PRESERVING SOME FOODS DURING LONG OCEAN CROSSINGS. (SIMILARLY ONE RECALLS THE RENOWNED VINEGAR FROM TOURS WHICH WAS REALLY GOOD WINE FROM BORDEAUX WHICH SOMETIMES TURNED TO VINEGAR HALF-WAY TO PARIS, IN THE VICINITY OF TOURS!) THIS RECIPE FROM PORTUGAL SOMEHOW AFFILIATED ITSELF WITH SAFFRON IN INDIA AND FOUND ITS WAY TO OUR SHORES. OUR VINDYE ALSO BASED ON VINEGAR, GARLIC, SAFFRON, AND OTHER SPICES, IS AN EXCELLENT WAY TO PREPARE AND PRESERVE FISH AND MEATS (BEEF, PORK AND VENISON).

THE INDIAN DISH CHICKEN VINDALOO (SEE RECIPE) HAS THE SAME ETIOLOGY. HERE IT TURNED INTO A WICKEDLY SPICED DISH!

# CALAMARY "PETITE MARIE"

## INGREDIENTS : 8 TO 10 SERVINGS

6 lbs calamary (squid), or octopus

1 piece fresh ginger, peeled

$1/2$ cup oil

2 dozen small shrimps, whole

2 lbs ripe tomatoes, or pommes d'amour, chopped

1 small can tomato purée

1 clove garlic

2 shallots

1 teaspoon salt

Pepper

Boil the calamary, or octopus, with ginger for two hours, or until very tender. Drain, cut in one inch strips, and reserve. If octopus is used, peel skin and discard suction cups.

Heat the oil in a skillet, and sauté the shrimps until they turn pink. Remove from heat, cool, and peel, reserving tail meat. Put shrimp heads and shells in skillet, add one cup water, and boil for five minutes. Place mixture in a mortar or blender, and crush coarsely. Strain through a fine-meshed strainer or several layers of cheese-cloth, and reserve juice.

Place shrimp meat and juice in a food processor or blender. Add tomatoes, tomato purée, garlic, shallots, and salt. Blend to obtain a fine purée.

Heat the pureed mixture in a saucepan. Add the calamary, or octopus meat, and cook for 15 minutes.

**MARIE DARUTY DE GRANDPRÉ**

# Tartare des Îles

### Ingredients : 2 servings

400 gms fresh fish filets (preferably tuna or capitaine or babonne)

1 pinch of salt

2 tablespoon of olive oil virgin extra

2 young onions (échalottes)

1 pinch of pepper

2 pommes d'amour

Cut the fish and the emptied pomme d'amour in small cubes. Chop thinly the echalotte. Mix thoroughly with all other ingredients. Add to your taste some fresh ginger thinly grinded.

Serve cold. We suggest that this tartare be put on a bed of salad of fresh heart palm.

Dress with thin layers of dried coconut and lettuce.

Pipo  LENOIR

# ROUGAIL OF SALTED FISH (OR SNOEK)

Salted snoek with its firm, rich, and tasty flesh comes to us from South Africa. The snoek, unfortunately, is not part of the abundant Mauritian marine fauna.

## INGREDIENTS

$^{1}/_{2}$ lb snoek
5 tablespoons oil

Cut the snoek in pieces and put to soak for 30 minutes. Drain and pat dry. Fry over medium heat for 15 minutes, place over paper towels to absorb any excess oil, and add to rougail sauce towards the end of cooking.

*NOTE: Other salted fish such as the licorne (known to local fishermen as poisson corne) can be substituted in the above recipe. The licorne has no scales, but a tough skin which must be removed. Not as tender as the snoek, it needs to be soaked for several hours.*

*Another candidate is the whole dried cordonnier, or its salted fillets. The fish, cut in pieces, or the fillets are fried briefly - 2 or 3 minutes. The fillets are in fact very lightly salted and taste almost like fresh fish. One half fillet will usually suffice per person, but take into account the appetites of your guests.*

*"ROUGAIL" SAUCE - The following is a basic recipe used whenever a "Rougail" (or Rougaille) is called for. The proportion of the ingredients may vary to suit the main element in each dish.*

$1^{3}/_{4}$ lbs (750 grams) very ripe tomatoes or "belles pommes d'amour"
4 tablespoons oil
1 onion, thinly sliced
1 teaspoon turmeric (optional)
5 large cloves garlic, crushed
1 small piece ginger root, crushed
Thyme and parsley
1 cup water
Salt and pepper

## OPTIONAL:

5 leaves curry leaves ("carripoulé")
2 or 3 long fresh chillies (cut in half lengthwise)

Chop the tomatoes, or process them briefly in a food processor.

Heat the oil. Add the onion and turmeric, and fry until onion starts to brown. Add the garlic and ginger, and cook for one minute. Stir in the tomatoes, thyme and parsley (plus the optional ingredients if desired) and cook over high heat for about 5 minutes, stirring so that mixture does not stick to the pan. Stir in about $^{1}/_{4}$ cup of water and let simmer for 5 to 6 minutes more until sauce is unctuous and has turned bright scarlet. Season with salt and pepper.

**JEAN-PIERRE LENOIR**

ROUGAIL (OUROUGAIL): THE DISH IS APPARENTLY OF TAMIL ORIGIN. IT APPEARS THAT THE TOMATO OR POMME D'AMOUR, WHICH WAS INTRODUCED IN FRANCE IN THE MIDDLE OF THE 17TH CENTURY, WAS ALMOST TOTALLY IGNORED IN THE CUISINE OF CHINA AND INDIA. THE OCCURRENCE OF ITS NUMEROUS USES IN MAURITIAN COOKERY MAY BE AN INFLUENCE WHICH TRAVELLED FROM WEST TO EAST. POSSIBLY FROM MADAGASCAR. THE MAURITIAN ROUGAIL IS A TOMATO BASED SAUCE IN WHICH IS SIMMERED SUCH INGREDIENTS AS SCALLIONS, SALT MEATS, AND FISH. IN REUNION THE TERM ROUGAIL IS EXCLUSIVELY USED FOR CHUTNEY - THE LATTER TERM IS ABSENT FROM THEIR CULINARY

# MOURGATE FRICASSÉ WITH POMMES D'AMOUR

The mourgate is a variety of calamary, weighing three kilos or more. Its milky white flesh is tough when raw, but becomes tender and tasty when cooked. It must be cleaned with care. Its single flat bone is removed, and the eyes, ink pocket, and guts are discarded. The outer mauvish membrane is peeled, or scraped off to reveal the perfectly white meat. It needs a sojourn of 12 or more hours in the freezer, followed by defrosting at room temperature, prior to cooking.

### INGREDIENTS : 8 SERVINGS

3 lbs mourgate
3/4 cup dry white wine
4 cups water
1 cup chicken bouillon
6 tablespoons chopped onion
1 large bouquet thyme and parsley
Salt and pepper

### SAUCE :

4 tablespoons vegetable oil
5 tablespoons chopped onion
1 1/2 tablespoons brandy
1/2 cup crushed ripe tomatoes, seeded
2 tablespoons tomato purée
1 1/2 teaspoons, each, crushed garlic and ginger
2 tablespoons chopped parsley
1 teaspoon leaf thyme
1/2 teaspoon sugar
1/4 teaspoon turmeric powder
Salt and pepper

Place the cleaned mourgate, wine, water, chicken bouillon, onion, herbs, salt and pepper in a pressure cooker. Cook over moderate heat for one hour from the time steam starts to escape.

Drain the mourgate, and cut into one centimetre strips. Discard the bouquet of herbs from cooking juice, and boil until reduced to a thick sauce. Reserve.

In a saucepan heat the oil. Add the onion and sauté until wilted and transparent. Stir in the mourgate strips and the brandy and flambé. Add the tomatoes and cook over high heat for about four minutes, stirring. Add the rest of the ingredients, plus the reserved cooking juice. Season to taste, and cook for 15 minutes, uncovered, stirring occasionally. If sauce becomes too thick, add water as needed to maintain it at the consistency of thick cream.

Mound a circle of buttered rice on a pre-heated platter. Ladle the fricassée in the centre, sprinkle with parsley, and serve immediately.

RAYMOND DE RAVEL

# ROULADES OF SMOKED MARLIN WITH HEART OF PALM

*The blue marlin, commonly known in Mauritius as empereur, is smoked on the island. The Mauritian smoked Marlin is delicate in taste and texture, and has an attractive pale orange colour similar to smoked salmon. Smoked marlin makes an elegant hors d'oeuvre or first course for festive occasions. The following recipe, easily executed, is suitable for more formal dinners or for banquets, and works equally well with smoked salmon.*

## INGREDIENTS : 4 SERVINGS

8 thin slices, approx. 3 x 6 inches, smoked marlin

1 fresh heart of palm

4 cups of milk

## HOLLANDAISE SAUCE :

$1/2$ lb unsalted chilled butter

3 egg yolks

1 tablespoon vinegar or lemon juice

Salt and freshly ground pepper

Boil the heart of palm in the four cups of milk with a little salt. Add water as needed to fully cover the heart of palm. Cook for one hour, or until tender when pierced with a fork. Remove from cooking liquid, and cool.

*Hollandaise sauce :*

In a small saucepan, place the egg yolks, vinegar or lemon juice, and ground pepper. Set over a larger pan of boiling water off the fire, and start beating the egg yolks. Continue beating while adding the butter, one tablespoon at a time until all the butter is absorbed. The sauce should be thick and unctuous like a mayonnaise. Season to taste with salt and set pan over hot water to keep sauce warm, stirring occasionally.

## NOTE :

At no point should the water in the bottom pan boil since this will cause the sauce to curdle.

Cut two four-inch cylinders from the heart of palm. Divide these in four pieces each, lengthwise. Wrap a piece of smoked marlin around each piece, and place on a serving platter. Nap generously with hollandaise sauce and garnish with watercress, lettuce leaves, or parsley. Serve immediately.

**RAYMOND DE RAVEL**

# OYSTERS IN PUFF PASTRY

## INGREDIENTS : 4 SERVINGS

60 Mauritian oysters or
24 medium-size oysters
2 tablespoons dry white wine
1 teaspoon sweet Sherry (Xères) or port
1 tablespoon butter

### SAUCE :

4 tablespoons minced onion
4 tablespoons crème fraîche
$1/2$ lb butter
$1/4$ cup dry white wine
Salt and pepper
$3/4$ lb puff pastry dough
1 egg yolk mixed with 2 tablespoons water

Shuck the oysters and place them in a bowl. Strain juices through a fine meshed strainer, and add to oysters with the wine and sherry. Reserve.

### THE SAUCE :

In a small saucepan, melt butter and add the onion. Cook over low heat, stirring frequently until transparent. Add white wine and two tablespoons of the oyster juice and cook over high heat, stirring, until sauce is reduced to the consistency of thick cream.

Stir in the crème fraîche and season to taste – since the oyster juice is already salty, add salt very carefully. Simmer for about 10 minutes until sauce thickens to the consistency of a mayonnaise.

Remove from heat, and beat in the butter one tablespoon at a time, waiting until each is absorbed before adding the next. The sauce should be extremely suave. Keep it warm, over a bowl of medium hot water, stirring occasionally. Do not reheat sauce because it is bound to curdle.

### THE PASTRY :

Provide yourself with the best puff pastry available, unless you have the patience and skill to make your own. On a lightly floured board, roll out dough until it is one inch thick. Cut out six rectangular pieces 3 x 6 inches. Place them on a lightly buttered and floured baking sheet. Brush tops with beaten egg yolk, taking care not to let any drip over the sides of the rectangles. Place on the upper middle shelf in a pre-heated 425° oven for about 15 minutes, until puffed and golden. Watch carefully, and remove at once if pastry starts to scorch on top. Slice each shell in two horizontally, using a sharp knife.

In a skillet, heat one tablespoon butter. Add the reserved oysters and juices, and poach for two minutes. Remove from heat. Place the bottom half of the pastry shells on the plates. Top with the oysters, dividing them equally. Spoon generously with sauce, and cover with tops of pastry shells. Serve immediately.

Six pastry shells are advised for four persons because most people will readily ask for more ... For big eaters you may wish to increase this to eight portions.

**RAYMOND DE RAVEL**

# OYSTER CANAPÉS

## INGREDIENTS : 8 TO 10 SERVINGS

100 Mauritian oysters*

Salt and pepper

5 tablespoons oil

1 small onion, thinly sliced

1 bouquet garni (thyme, parsley)

2 tablespoons flour

2 cups milk

$1^1/_2$ bread, "pain de mie" or other dense white bread, cut into slices and deep fried

* Mauritian oysters are wonderfully tasty, but very small. It takes 3 or 4 of those to equal one medium size European or American oyster.

Shuck the oysters. Wash in sea water, if possible, to remove any sand or bits of oyster shells. Sprinkle with a little salt and some freshly ground pepper.

Heat the oil in a skillet. Sauté the onions until golden. Add the herbs, cook briefly to impart flavour, and discard. Add the flour and cook, stirring, until the mixture bubbles. Add the oysters, cook for one minute, then pour in the milk, a little at a time, until completely absorbed, and stirring gently but continuously. Adjust seasonings.

Spoon the oysters on the fried bread slices and serve hot.

JACQUELINE DALAIS

# CAMARONS À LA SAUCE ROUGE

## INGREDIENTS : 4 TO 5 SERVINGS

30  (about 3 lbs) camarons - fresh water prawns

1 lb of small river shrimps

5 tablespoons oil

1 small onion, thinly sliced

1 ripe tomato

Sprig of parsley

Salt and pepper

Heat four tablespoons of oil and sauté the camarons with a tablespoon of water until they turn bright red. Remove from heat and let cool for a few minutes. Separate heads from tails by twisting gently. Peel the tail sections and reserve meat. Discard eyes, then crush the heads, legs, and tail shells. Place in a saucepan with just enough water to cover the crushed shells and boil for a few minutes together with the purée of river shrimps previously crushed in a mixer with little water. Reserve.

Heat the remaining oil and brown the onion. Add the reserved broth, tomato, parsley, salt and pepper. Simmer until reduced to the consistency of light cream, then strain. Transfer sauce to a saucepan with the reserved tail meat and simmer gently for about 10 minutes until the sauce thickens. Adjust seasonings, and serve very hot.

Camarons with "sauce rouge" can be served over rounds of cooked hearts of palm or over hot croûtons. The dish may also be served surrounded with a ring of fluffy buttered rice.

JEAN-PIERRE LENOIR

# ISLAND STYLE CRAB SALAD

## INGREDIENTS : 8 TO 10 SERVINGS

2 lbs  crab meat (more or less crabs, small or large, to yield 2 lbs)

3 ripe pommes d'amour or tomatoes

1 bouquet thyme and parsley

1 small chopped onion

2 to 3 tablespoons olive oil

## SAUCE :

1 hard-boiled egg, chopped

10 to 12 scallions or chives

1 pinch mustard

1 teaspoon sugar

Tabasco or chillies to taste

1 tablespoon olive oil

1 lemon

Salt and pepper

## GARNISH :

8 lettuce leaves

sliced tomatoes, hard-boiled eggs, and lemons

black olives

Cut the live crabs in quarters. Rinse in cold water and discard the upper shell and the underside plate. Clean them well. Place crabs in a saucepan with the pommes d'amour, herbs, onion, and olive oil. Bring to a boil, and cook briefly until the crabs turn red. Remove, cool, and pick all the crab meat from the shells.

Make a sauce from the listed ingredients and season it. Mix in the crab meat.

Arrange the lettuce leaves on a platter. Place some of the crab salad on each leaf and decorate as desired. Serve chilled.

# LOBSTER A LA SAUCE VIVI

## INGREDIENTS : 8 TO 10 SERVINGS

8 lbs spiny lobsters

## SAUCE :

2 egg yolks

Pinch of mustard powder

4 tablespoons oil

$1/2$ teaspoon sugar

Salt, pepper and Tabasco — to taste

1 lemon, squeezed

6 tablespoons heavy cream, or 5 tablespoons powdered milk dissolved in a little water

2 shallots, minced

Plunge lobsters in boiling water and cook 30 minutes, or four minutes per lb of lobster — timing starts when water comes back to a boil. When cooked, drain lobsters, and detach heads from tails. (The lobster heads, combined with eggplant, can be used to make a curry). Remove lobster meat from shells, and discard the dorsal vein. Cut into one to one and a half inch slices and arrange on a platter.

Sauce :

Place the egg yolks, mustard, and oil in a bowl. Beat with a spatula until homogeneous, but without making a mayonnaise. Season with half teaspoon sugar, salt, pepper, crouton, and the lemon juice. Mix well, and then beat in the cream and the shallots.

Pour sauce over the lobster slices, and create an attractive decoration with optional garnishes.

VIVIAN DE  ROQUEFEUIL-NOËL

# LOBSTER MEDAILLONS WITH ORANGE HONEY

## INGREDIENTS : 10 SERVINGS

8 lbs of lobster

5 tablespoons honey

1/2 cup vinegar

10 oranges

1/2 lbs butter

Pinch of cayenne pepper

Salt and pepper

## GARNISH:

6 oranges, bouquet of parsley,

2 or 3 tomatoes, cut into small dice

Choose fresh and lively lobsters. Cook them in a seasoned court-bouillon for 15 minutes. Remove and keep in a cool place.

### THE ORANGE SAUCE:

Heat the honey and vinegar over low heat. Cook for a few minutes until the mixture is slightly reduced. Add the juice of 10 oranges and cook until three quarter reduced. Just before serving beat in the butter and season with cayenne pepper.

### GARNISH:

Peel off the zest of 4 oranges and cut into fine juliennes. Blanch them for 5 minutes in boiling water. Peel and section all the oranges. You will need 60 sections: 6 per plate. Discard all the inner membranes.

### PRESENTATION OF THE PLATES:

Extract the tail meat from the lobsters and slice them into "médaillons". You will need 70 slices: 7 per plate. Calculate accordingly before slicing.

Sauté the medallions very briefly in butter so that they are just warm. Nap the plates with the orange honey sauce. Place one médaillon in the centre of each plate, and alternate one médaillon and one orange segment in a circle around it.

# GRATIN OF SPINY LOBSTER IN RED SAUCE

### INGREDIENTS : 4 SERVINGS

2 to 3 lbs spiny lobster

1/3 cup dry white wine

3 tablespoons water

4 tablespoons peanut or sunflower oil

4 tablespoons minced onion

6 very ripe pommes d'amour or

3 ripe tomatoes, chopped

2 tablespoons tomato purée

1 tablespoon chopped parsley

1 teaspoon thyme leaves

1 tablespoon cognac or brandy

### BECHAMEL SAUCE :

3 tablespoons butter

1 cup flour

2 cups cold milk

2 egg yolks

4 tablespoons grated cheese (Gruyère, Gouda or Cheddar)

Cut the lobsters in half lengthwise. Discard the insides, including spongy gills, digestive tract, etc ... Place in a pot with white wine and three tablespoons water, cover, and cook for 15 to 20 minutes, depending on the size of the lobsters, until shells are bright scarlet. Remove lobsters, and reserve cooking liquid.

Shell lobsters, and extract as much meat as possible from heads and legs. Cut tails into 1/2 inch rounds. Place in a bowl, cover with plastic wrap and reserve. Crush shells and heads coarsely, mix with two cups water, and boil for five minutes, stirring. Strain broth into a glass bowl, and let stand for a while before using to allow any small particles to settle at the bottom.

### RED SAUCE :

In a saucepan heat the oil, add onions and let cook over low heat until transparent. Add the pommes d'amour, tomato purée, parsley and thyme. Cook for five to six minutes, then pour in the reserved cooking juice, and one cup of the broth. Boil until sauce is reduced to the consistency of light cream. Season to taste, cook for five more minutes, and add in the lobster meat and cognac or brandy. Mix well, and boil for another 10 to 15 minutes. The sauce is ready when it is thick and unctuous. Remove from heat and reserve.

### BECHAMEL :

Place butter and flour in a saucepan. Heat, stirring, until mixture starts to bubble and turns golden. Add the milk all at once, and stir vigorously while mixture comes to a boil. Remove from heat, beat in two tablespoons of grated cheese and the egg yolks, and adjust seasonings.

Butter a shallow oven-proof dish. Spoon half of the bechamel sauce on the bottom, cover evenly with the lobster mixture, and top with the rest of the bechamel sauce. Sprinkle with the rest of the cheese, and place in a 400° pre-heated oven for 15 to 20 minutes. The dish is ready when the top turns crusty and golden brown. Serve immediately.

**RAYMOND DE RAVEL**

# FRICASSEE OF "PIPENGAILLES" AND SHRIMP

## INGREDIENTS : 6 TO 8 SERVINGS

$^1/_4$ lb dried shrimp (available in oriental markets)

4 lbs pipengailles

2 tablespoons oil

1 small onion

$^1/_2$ teaspoon turmeric

3 cloves garlic, crushed

1 or 2 small ripe tomatoes, chopped

4 curry leaves

1 cup water

Thyme and parsley salt and pepper

Chilli, a dash (optional)

Place the dried shrimps to soak in warm water for one hour.

Peel the pipengailles and cut them into slices.

Heat the oil in a skillet and sauté the onions until lightly browned. Add the turmeric, garlic and tomatoes and cook for one or two minutes over high heat. Stir in the pipengailles and the drained shrimps. Cook for five minutes over medium heat, stirring. Stir in the remaining ingredients and cook, covered, for about 10 minutes, stirring occasionally. To reduce, cook sauce a few more minutes uncovered.

### NOTE:

*Pipengailles, also "pipengayes", are elongated, ridged squash with a delicate, almost sweet taste. They are also called pleated squash, Chinese okra, or sponge gourd. The skin is sometimes used to make chutney.*

*Pipengailles can also be used in pork curries, or gratinéed with bechamel sauce.*

# Meats, Poultry, Venison

# BREDES DE CHINE (INDIAN MUSTARD GREENS) WITH FATBACK

## INGREDIENTS : 4 TO 6 SERVINGS

1 1/4 lbs brèdes de Chine leaves

1/2 lb salt pork or fatback

1/2 chicken bouillon cube

4 tablespoons sunflower or peanut oil

4 tablespoons chopped onion

1 teaspoon crushed garlic

1 teaspoon crushed ginger root

2 tablespoons water

Salt and pepper

> **BREDES** - A BOUILLON MADE WITH LEAVES AND TENDER SHOOTS OF CERTAIN PLANTS, VEGETABLES, OR CREEPERS. IT IS USED TO WET RICE. BRÈDES ARE ALSO MADE IN **ÉTOUFFÉES** I.E. COOKED WITHOUT WATER. (SEE RECIPES). WE BELIEVE THIS DISH WAS AN IMPORT FROM THE MALAGASY REPUBLIC.

Cut the brèdes de Chine leaves into two inch sections, and wash them well.

Clean the piece of salt pork or fat back, scraping and washing well to remove any surface brine. Cut into half cubes, blanch in boiling water for three to four minutes, and drain.

Heat the oil in a saucepan. Add the pork and onions, and cook gently until lightly browned. Stir in the half bouillon cube, the garlic, ginger and water. Season lightly, keeping in mind that the bouillon cube and pork are already salty. Stir and cook briefly before adding the brèdes. Bring to a simmer and cook for 15 to 20 minutes, stirring occasionally.

## NOTE :

*This delicious dish is served very hot over rice with any meat curry, all rougails and all fricassées. I have also served it with roasts (beef or pork) and found the combination most agreeable.*

*This recipe can also be made using "Malabar" leaves, or a mixture of "Malabar" with christophene or pumpkin shoots. In either case the leaves should be weighed after the stems have been discarded.*

**RAYMOND DE RAVEL**

# BRÈDES SONGES AND DHOLL

The Songes plants grow in thick, luxuriant clumps along the banks of Mauritian rivers and streams, and in marshy areas. In the Caribbean region, this plant is known as either callaloo or elephant's ear. The leaves, which can grow to be 2 to 3 feet long, are somewhat heart-shaped. Several varieties of "Songes" exist. Most are simply decorative and presumably poisonous; of the only two that are edible, one type has shiny dark green leaves and burgundy tinted stems, while the other has leaves and stems of the palest green.

### INGREDIENTS : 5 TO 6 SERVINGS

1 lb dholl (red or yellow lentils)
3 lbs brèdes Songes
4 tablespoons oil
1 small onion, chopped
$1/4$ lb ripe tomatoes, seeded and chopped
1 clove garlic, crushed
1 branch fresh thyme or 1 teaspoon leaf thyme
1 long green chilli (or more as desired)
1 tablespoon tamarind paste or 4 tablespoons vinegar
3 cups water
Salt and pepper

Place the dholl in a bowl, cover with cold water, and let soak for two hours or overnight. Drain.
Shred the Songe leaves. Peel and chop the stems.
Heat the oil, add the onions, and sauté until wilted. Add the tomatoes, garlic, thyme and chilli and cook over high heat, stirring, for two minutes. Stir in the tamarind paste or vinegar, the dholl*, the brèdes, and the water. Cover the saucepan, and let simmer for about one hour (or cook for 30 to 40 minutes in a pressure cooker).

* The dholl can be boiled separately and added to the brèdes halfway through the cooking.

*VARIATIONS:* Brèdes Songes can be combined with "Chevrettes" (small fresh water shrimps), and salted fish or pork. Fry the "Chevrettes" briefly and add to the brèdes Songes halfway through the cooking. Add the desalted fish or pork (cut into cubes and fried) in the same manner.

### BRÈDES SONGES WITH PORK OR BEEF:

Substitute $1 1/2$ lbs lean pork or beef for the dholl and add no water. Cut the meat into small cubes and fry until well browned before adding to the dish.

### NOTE OF WARNING:

"Songes" is the strongest tasting of all the brèdes: you will either love it or hate it! "Songes" may cause an allergic itching reaction in some people; tamarind and vinegar are said to be the antidotes and are conveniently included in the recipe! This could be construed as a double warning ...

# BITTER MELON AND SALT PORK

**INGREDIENTS : 6 TO 8 SERVINGS**

3 lbs bitter melons (margozes)

$^1/_4$ lb salt pork, or fatback

4 tablespoons oil, or lard

1 onion, finely sliced

1 or 2 ripe tomatoes

Salt and pepper

Scrape the bitter melons thoroughly on the outside. Cut them in half lengthwise, remove the seeds, then scrape on the inside. Plunge in boiling water, remove, drain, and reserve.

Cut the salt pork in little cubes and fry in the oil. Add the onions, the tomatoes, a few tablespoons of boiling water, and the bitter melons. Season with salt and pepper and let simmer for 15 to 20 minutes.

**M. JAUFFRET**

# BRIANI

## INGREDIENTS : 10 SERVINGS

1.5 kgs of lamb (or mutton)

4 lbs basmati rice

20 medium potatoes

10 large onions cut into slices

4 plain yoghurts

25 gms garlic

20 gms ginger

3 tablespoons oil

10 gms cinnamon

3 cloves

10 gms cardamom

10 gms aniseed

5 green chillis (optional)

1 tablespoon saffron

1 teaspoon chilli powder

Salt and pepper

In a large pan, fry onion and potatoes until golden brown in one tablespoon vegetable oil together with three teaspoons salt, one teaspoon chilli powder. Add cinnamon, cloves, pepper, cardamom and aniseed. Set aside.

In a large pan, fry lamb cut into pieces with two tablespoons vegetable oil, three teaspoons salt, garlic, ginger, until lamb is brown. Set aside.

Add onions and potatoes, saffron, plain yoghurts, four to five green chillis (optional), coriander.

Leave for half an hour.

In a large pan, boil water with 10 teaspoons of salt.

As soon as it starts boiling, turn off fire and let it cool in water for 5 to 6 minutes.

Drain rice and arrange over lamb mixture.

Pour saffron over rice.

Seal lid of saucepan with foil paper and cook slowly for half an hour.

**CATHERINE MAYER**

---

**BRIANI (BRYANI):** TYPICAL MUSLIM DISH - PORK THEREFORE IS FORBIDDEN AS IS BEEF AMONG HINDUS. THE DIVERSITY OF SPICES USED MAKES FOR A RICH SAVOURY DISH.

# DRY CURRY

### INGREDIENTS : 6 SERVINGS

2 lbs lean and tender beef

6 tablespoons oil

1 lb onions, cut in thick slices

6 tablespoons finely minced onion

2 tablespoons curry powder

1 cup water

1 bouquet thyme and parsley

3 tablespoons raisins soaked in rum

1 cup small fried croutons

2 tablespoons finely chopped parsley

Salt and pepper

Cut the beef into one inch cubes. Heat the oil in a saucepan and sauté the onions over high heat until they are golden brown. Remove from pan and reserve.

In the same pan, brown the beef and minced onion in the hot oil for 5 minutes. Add the curry powder, one cup water, and the herb bouquet. Season with salt and pepper, and simmer until meat is tender. Reduce any remaining sauce until all liquid evaporates and only the oil is left. At this point the curry will be dry, but unctuous.

Add the drained raisins to the curry and cook over low heat for 5 more minutes. Just prior to serving mix the croutons gently in the curry, top with the reserved onions and sprinkle with parsley.

In true creole fashion, serve this dry curry with a platter of basmati rice, a chutney of coconut, and another of pommes d'amour.

**RAYMOND DE RAVEL**

# CURRIED PORK WITH HEART OF PALM

## INGREDIENTS : 6 SERVINGS

2 lbs lean pork

4 tablespoons oil

fresh ground pepper to taste

1 medium onion, finely chopped

$1/4$ lb very ripe pommes d'amour or tomatoes, chopped

1 tablespoon fresh turmeric root, crushed

(or 2 teaspoons turmeric powder)

$1/2$ teaspoon crushed ginger root

$1/2$ teaspoon chopped thyme

1 tablespoon chopped parsley

$3/4$ cup water

1 fresh heart of palm – if unavailable use 2x1-lb can.

Salt and pepper

Cut the pork in $1/2$ inch cubes and sprinkle with pepper. Heat the oil, add the pork, and cook over medium heat until browned – about 20 minutes. Remove pork and reserve. In the same pan, sauté onions until wilted. Add the tomatoes and cook over high heat for two to three minutes. Stir in the turmeric, ginger, thyme, and parsley, and then add the reserved pork and $3/4$ cup water. Cook, stirring, for two to three minutes, remove from heat, and reserve.

Prepare the heart of palm and boil, covered, in the milk and water mixture about 20 minutes, until slightly crunchy. Cut into one inch slices.

Add the heart of palm to the pork, placing the slices delicately on top. Without stirring, spoon the sauce evenly to cover them, and simmer for 10 minutes. Transfer to a platter, placing the heart of palm in the centre and the sauce all around. Garnish with sprigs of parsley.

Serve accompanied with bowls of rice and delicately spiced chutneys.

PHILIPPE LENOIR

# CHICKEN MULUGATAWNY
# (OR MOULOUKTANY)

## INGREDIENTS : 8 SERVINGS

1 chicken weighing about 3 lbs

$^1/_2$ ripe coconut with its water

2 tablespoons curry powder dissolved in 4 lts water

2 tablespoons tamarind paste

3 tablespoons oil

1 medium onion, chopped

$^1/_2$ lb very ripe pommes d'amour or tomatoes, chopped

2 tablespoons chopped parsley

1 teaspoon chopped thyme

1 teaspoon crushed ginger root

1 teaspoon small chillies, crushed

2 chicken bouillon cubes dissolved in one cup boiling water

Salt and pepper


Roast the chicken until done, but not dry. Separate into pieces.

Grate the coconut and mix into two cups warm water. Stir well, then strain through a cloth, pressing well to extract all the juice. Dissolve the tamarind paste in the coconut water, then strain.

Heat the oil and sauté the onions until lightly browned. Add the tomatoes and cook over high heat for about five minutes. Add the parsley, thyme, ginger, garlic, chillies, and the curry powder. Stir well, then add the chicken. Cook for one or two minutes and add the tamarind and chicken bouillon. Cook for 10 to 15 minutes. Serve accompanied with rice and a choice of chutneys: coconut, tomato, eggplant etc ...

### J. ROGER MONTOCCHIO

MULLIGATAWNY (MOULOUKTANI - "MUGLI TANNIR"): ORIGINATED IN THE SOUTH OF INDIA. IT IS A HIGHLY SPICED SOUP OR BOUILLON, MADE WITH MEATS, POULTRY, OR SHELLFISH - FREQUENTLY UTILIZING LEFTOVERS.

# PILAW OF CHICKEN AND PORK

## INGREDIENTS

1 cut-up chicken of 2$^1$/$_2$ to 3 lbs

1 to 2 tablespoons oil

1 lb lean fresh pork, or blanched salted pork –
viande salée – cut in $^1$/$_2$ inch cubes

1 lb pork sausages

3 tablespoons oil

2 medium onions, chopped

1 tablespoon crushed garlic

1 bouquet thyme and parsley

1 tablespoon turmeric (for a deeper colour use more)

1 lb pommes d'amour or tomatoes, chopped or passed through a food mill

1 small piece cinnamon bark or $^1$/$_4$ teaspoon powder

4 whole cloves

2 long chillies

6 cups chicken stock or bouillon

2$^1$/$_2$ lbs rice

Salt and freshly ground pepper

## GARNISH :

2 bell peppers

In a large saucepan, heat the oil, and sauté in turn until nicely browned, the chicken pieces, the pork, and the sausages. Reserve and keep warm.

In the same saucepan heat the three tablespoons of oil. Add the onions, garlic, and herbs and sauté until onions are wilted but not browned. Add the turmeric, pommes d'amour purée, cinnamon, cloves, and chillies. Cook, stirring, for 4 to 5 minutes.

### OPTIONAL :

Make a stock with six cups of water and the chicken carcass, wings, neck, and gizzard. Or use six cups of chicken bouillon for the next step.

Add the chicken stock or bouillon to the saucepan. Stir and then add the rice (previously well rinsed). Bring to a boil, and simmer over low heat for 40 to 50 minutes. Half-way through the cooking, add the reserved chicken, pork, and sausages. Watch carefully so the rice grains are cooked through but not sticky. Garnish with sliced bell peppers.

Serve with a dish of brèdes – bouillon or étouffée – and with a variety of chutneys: pommes d'amour, eggplant, coconut etc … Fried croutons will add a nice, crunchy touch to the pilaw.

---

**PILAU (PILAW, PILAU, PULLAO):** RICE DISH COLOURED WITH TURMERIC (SAFFRON OF THE INDIES) OR CURRY POWDER, REDOLENT OF SPICES AND MADE WITH OR WITHOUT MEAT. OF PERSIAN ORIGIN, THE DISH CAME TO US FROM INDIA AND IS LOCALLY CALLED "PLOT", WITH A SILENT "T".

# CHICKEN CURRY WITH FRESH SAFFRON

*Fresh Saffron (safran vert) used here is the root of the turmeric plant. It is also known as Saffron of the Indies. It bears no relation to Spanish saffron which is the dried stamen of the cultivated crocus.*

### INGREDIENTS : 4 TO 5 SERVINGS

1 chicken weighing 3 lbs, cut into pieces

4 tablespoons oil

1 medium onion, finely chopped

1 teaspoon each crushed garlic and ginger

$1/4$ lb very ripe pommes d'amour or tomatoes, crushed

1 teaspoon turmeric powder

3 tablespoons crushed fresh saffron root

4 to 5 leaves curry leaves

$1/2$ cup water

Thyme, parsley, salt and pepper

Sauté the chicken in hot oil until golden (about 10 minutes), Remove to a side dish and reserve. In the same pan, sauté onions, garlic and ginger. Add the tomatoes, turmeric, and fresh saffron root crushed on the curry stone or in a mortar. Stir, and add the curry leaves, salt and pepper. Cook over medium heat for 6 to 7 minutes. Add the chicken and half cup water (more if you prefer a runny sauce), mix well, and cover. Cook for 20 minutes or until chicken is done.

Fresh saffron root imparts a lovely golden colour to the curry. If unavailable use twice as much turmeric. As for the curry leaves (or "4 épices" leaves) they lend an exotic flavour to any dish; unfortunately they can be hard to locate in unexotic climates!

### NOTE :

*The same recipe can be used to make a light and pleasant curry with beef, pork, fish or crustacean.*

**PHILIPPE LENOIR**

# CHICKEN GESIERS WITH SNAIL BUTTER AND OYSTER MUSHROOMS

## INGREDIENTS : 4 TO 6 SERVINGS

1 lb chicken gizzards (gesiers)

3 tablespoons finely minced shallots

1 teaspoon thyme leaves

2 tablespoons finely minced parsley

$1/2$ chicken bouillon cube

3 large cloves garlic, finely minced

5 cups water

$1^1/2$ cups dry white wine

1 tablespoon butter

1 tablespoon olive oil

1 can oyster mushrooms, drained and cut in fine strips

Salt and pepper

## SNAIL BUTTER :

1 lb butter

2 cloves garlic, finely minced

2 tablespoons finely chopped parsley

Wash the gizzards thoroughly. Slice across the fleshy part and remove the tough outer rind of the gizzards. Place them in a pressure cooker with the shallots, thyme, parsley, half the bouillon cube, garlic, and water. Start timing when pressure cooker starts whistling and cook for one hour.

Remove lid of cooker and add the white wine, butter, olive oil, and oyster mushrooms. Cook, uncovered, until sauce is reduced to the consistency of thick cream. Season with salt and pepper.

Transfer mixture in a shallow dish, or better still in individual ramekins, and spread in a layer no more than one inch thick. Cool thoroughly.

Meanwhile, prepare the snail butter: stir the butter, garlic, and parsley until the mixture is homogeneous.

Spread the snail butter over the cold gizzards. Bake in a hot oven (425°) for 10 to 12 minutes and serve immediately.

RAYMOND DE RAVEL

# TANDOORI CHICKEN

<u>**INGREDIENTS :**</u>

1 3-lb chicken

1 tablespoon garam massala

1 teaspoon powdered chilli

(or less according to taste)

$^1/_2$ teaspoon nutmeg

2 cups natural yoghurt (unsweetened)

a few sprigs fresh mint or coriander, chopped

Salt and pepper

red colouring if desired


Cut the chicken into pieces. Mix the rest of the ingredients and add to the chicken. Mix well and marinate for 12 hours.

Heat the tandoori oven with wood charcoal for one hour. Place the chicken on skewers and grill in the tandoori until done. A home grill or barbecue may be used with excellent results.

Serve accompanied with a choice of vegetables, baked potatoes or faratas and chutneys.

**(RESTAURANT LA BONNE MARMITE)**

# ROAST DUCK WITH MANGO SAUCE

## INGREDIENTS : 4 SERVINGS

1 young duck weighing approx. 4 lbs

1 half-ripe mango, cut into fine juliennes

### MARINADE :

6 tablespoons minced onions

4 tablespoons grated carrots

1 tablespoon finely chopped parsley

4 tablespoons oil (sunflower)

1 tablespoon freshly ground pepper

1 tablespoon sweet wine or white Port

### MANGO SAUCE :

1 ripe mango

2 teaspoons honey

2 tablespoons mango chutney (commercially prepared)

$1/2$ chicken bouillon cube

2 sprigs parsley

the neck and wings of the duck, chopped

Salt and pepper

Select a young and tender duck, not overly fat. Mix the marinade ingredients in a bowl. Rub the duck thoroughly with this melange and pour the excess marinade all over the bird. Place the liver and gizzard inside the cavity, and marinate in the refrigerator for approximately 18 hours. Remove two hours before cooking.

Heat oven to 450°. Sprinkle the duck with salt and place it in a roasting pan on its side – wing up. Roast on one side for 10 minutes, then on the other for the next 10 minutes. Roast duck on its back for the last 10 minutes.

### MEANWHILE PREPARE THE MANGO SAUCE :

Peel the ripe mango, cut out its flesh, and place in a blender or food processor with one cup of water. Pulverize to obtain a thick liquid. Strain and place in a saucepan with the rest of the sauce ingredients. Bring the sauce to a boil, reduce heat, and simmer for one hour, stirring frequently. Add water as needed to keep sauce light and unctuous. Remove from heat and pass through a strainer, pressing well over the neck and wing pieces to extract all the juice. Place in a small saucepan with the half-ripe mango julienne. Reserve and keep warm.

Carve and debone the duck. Cut the meat, liver and gizzard into thin strips (about $1/2$ inch thick). Collect all the juices from the carcass, add to the roasting pan with 4 tablespoons boiling water, and deglaze the pan. Strain and add to the reserved mango sauce. Bring sauce to a boil and cook for two minutes.

Set the duck meat on a warmed platter. Pour hot sauce evenly on top, and serve immediately.

### SUGGESTED ACCOMPANIMENT :

Boiled new potatoes sautéed in butter and sprinkled with finely chopped parsley.

**RAYMOND DE RAVEL**

# ROAST DUCK, CHINESE STYLE (CANARD LAQUÉ)

*Canard Laqué – so named because the skin of the duck becomes very crisp and develops such a high sheen that it looks lacquered.*

### INGREDIENTS

1 large young duckling – about 4 lbs

1 teaspoon maltose

6 tablespoons hot water

Pour some boiling water over the duck and then dry it thoroughly. Dissolve the maltose in the hot water and, with a brush, apply the mixture carefully all over the duck. Hang the duck to dry for 4 hours.

Roast the duck in a preheated oven at 425°. This is usually done by hanging the duck with a hook to the top shelf of the oven – a platter is placed underneath to catch the cooking juices. Or place the duck on a rack in a large roasting pan.

After 10 minutes, turn the duck over and cook for another 10 minutes. Reduce temperature to 375° and cook for 40 more minutes.

Serve immediately while the duck's skin is crispy. Season the pan juices with salt, pepper, and parsley and serve separately.  Serve with sliced green vegetables, small rice pancakes and plum sauce.

RESTAURANT CHEZ MANUEL, ST. JULIEN

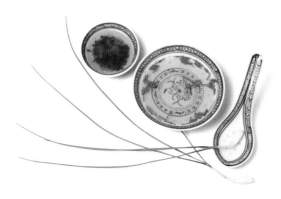

# RASSON

*Rasson is the Mauritian version of an Indian soup "Rasam" – a thin, fiery hot, lentil-based consommé. Rasson has a reputation for curing many ills, and in particular for combating the unpleasant physical effects of a hangover. Two bowls sipped the morning after, are guaranteed to make one stand up, ready to start anew! But Rasson is also a most agreeable addition to a meal of rice, beans and chutneys. It is frequently served at parties, usually after midnight, to be sipped slowly in genteel cups. It effectively chases yawns and galvanizes the guests so the party can go on!*

*This recipe for Rasson has been handed to us by Mme Manikon of Chamarel, wife of a well-known hunt tracker, who made barrels of the devilish brew on the feast of Saint Anne, patron saint of the parish. This tradition in olden times was made more interesting by a dose or two of illicit rum; a mere prank, a flouting of the law befitting the wild nature of this region of Black River.*

### INGREDIENTS : 10 TO 12 SERVINGS

$^1/_2$ lb dholl (yellow split peas)

1 lb brèdes Songes

4 tablespoons oil

1 medium onion, chopped

3 tablespoons ripe tamarind pulp

1 teaspoon crushed garlic

8 whole dried chillies

8 curry leaves

2 tablespoons chopped parsley

1 tablespoon chopped fresh coriander

1 teaspoon fresh or dried thyme leaves

1 or 2 whole cloves

1 teaspoon small aniseed, crushed

2 tablespoons turmeric

1 teaspoon black pepper

3 litres of water

Boil the dholl until creamy soft. Mix into a purée, and pass through a strainer. Reserve.

Cook the brèdes Songes until very tender, and crush in mixer.

Heat the oil in a large saucepan or stock pot. Add the onions and sauté until golden. Add the dholl, the brèdes and the tamarind. Let cook for 5 minutes. Add one cup of the water and all the spices, stirring well until the mixture is homogeneous. Bring to a boil, and cook for a few minutes before adding the rest of the water. Simmer, covered, for one hour.

Variations : Add to the Rasson, while it is cooking, the strained juice extracted from crushed lobster shells after they have been boiled.

Similarly, use the juice extracted from small crabs, or from the heads of shrimps or freshwater prawns (camarons).

Each ingredient contributes its specific flavour to the Rasson. The best Rasson, comments Mme Manikon, is made with a base of chicken stock and shellfish juices...

**MADAME MANIKON**

# MAURITIAN BRAISED VENISON

### INGREDIENTS : 6 TO 8 SERVINGS

5 lbs venison

2 cloves garlic, crushed

2 leaves "4 épices", chopped

2 shallots, finely minced

1 nutmeg, grated or 1 teaspoon powdered nutmeg

$1/4$ teaspoon cinnamon powder

$1/2$ teaspoon ground pepper

Thyme and salt to taste

6 tablespoons oil or 4 tablespoons cooking lard

4 carrots, thickly sliced

$1/4$ lb onions

1 beef bouillon

1 cube cup white wine

Mix together the "4 épices" leaves, shallots, nutmeg, cinnamon, pepper, thyme, and salt. Rub the venison thoroughly with this mixture.

Heat the cooking lard or oil. Add the meat, the carrots, and whole onions. Cook over medium heat, turning the meat over, until well browned on all sides. Add the bouillon cube and white wine, and cook covered for one hour.

**M. JAUFFRET**

# ROASTED RACK OF WILD BOAR
## (SANGLIER OR MARCASSIN)

### INGREDIENTS : 6 TO 8 SERVINGS

8 to 10 lbs rack of wild boar (one whole side of ribs)

2 cloves garlic, crushed

4 tablespoons oil

Thyme, parsley, salt and pepper


### MARINADE:

Oil, vinegar, garlic, sliced onions, thyme and freshly ground pepper


### GARNISH:

Croutons and parsley


Spoon the marinade over the rack of wild boar and baste it frequently over a period of about 12 hours. Using a sharp knife, cut through the rack transversely - without however completely separating the piece. Season with crushed garlic and sprinkle with thyme, chopped parsley, salt, and pepper. Baste the surfaces with oil and with the marinade juices. Place in a preheated 425° oven for about one hour, basting occasionally with the pan juices.

Remove from oven and cut the rack in half. Slice into serving pieces (two ribs per portion), and place on a heated platter. Garnish with croutons and parsley, and serve immediately.

JACQUES LENOIR

# SALMIS OF WILD BOAR WITH GREEN PEPPERCORNS

## INGREDIENTS : 8 SERVINGS

4 lbs wild boar meat (no bones)

1 tablespoon oil

1 teaspoon crushed garlic

3 tablespoons green peppercorns

2 oz or a small tin good grade liver pate

## MARINADE :

$1/2$ bottle dry red table wine

$1/4$ lb large onion

$1/4$ lb carrots, grated

3 tablespoons hot prepared mustard

1 tablespoon peppercorns

Cut the meat into large cubes and place in the marinade for 24 hours. When ready to cook, remove onions from marinade and sauté with garlic in one tablespoon oil. Cook for 5 minutes. Add meat, and brown over medium heat for 15 minutes. Stir in the marinade, green peppercorns, and thinly mixed paté. Cook, uncovered, for 30 minutes. Remove from heat. Serve with rice or a good purée (potatoes or, best, "arouille").

## NOTE :

*This recipe can also be made with venison.*

JEAN-PIERRE LENOIR

# JUGGED HARE "SAINT GEORGES"

### INGREDIENTS : 6 SERVINGS

One 3 lbs hare
1 pinch of muscade
1 bouquet thyme and parsley
50 gms shallots
2 cloves
1 tablespoon of cognac
$^1/_2$ bottle of good red wine
Salt and pepper

Cut the hare in serving pieces, reserving the liver and blood for the sauce.

Place the hare in a bowl and sprinkle with salt, black pepper, and a little grated nutmeg. Add a bouquet of thyme and parsley, a few bay leaves, some shallots, and two whole cloves. Sprinkle with a little cognac and pour in enough, or other good red wine, to completely cover the hare.

Let marinate for about 24 hours, turning the pieces over every few hours.

### TO COOK :

Remove the pieces of hare from the marinade and pat them dry. Heat three tablespoons butter in a heavy saucepan (preferably made of cast iron), add a few pieces of diced salt pork and one dozen pearl onions, and sauté until browned. Remove and transfer to a side dish. Add some more butter to the pan and sauté the pieces of hare until seared on all sides. Stir in some finely minced shallots and garlic, a bouquet of thyme and parsley, and adjust the seasonings.

### TO PREPARE THE SAUCE:

Bring the wine marinade to a rolling boil. Cook for a few minutes, then remove from heat and stir in the reserved liver (finely chopped), the browned salt pork, and the pearl onions. Mix in the reserved blood and season with salt and pepper. Add the sauce to the hare and simmer over low heat until the meat is very tender.

Transfer to a preheated serving dish, accompanied with croutons lightly seasoned with garlic.

PHILIPPE LENOIR

*N.B : This recipe became famous one night when a few friends joined after hunting. The only one bottle of wine they had to cook with was the very famous Chateau St. Georges. It was such a success that they called the dish after the name of the wine...*

# CIVET DE CHAUVE-SOURIS
## (STEW OF FLYING-FOX BAT)

### INGREDIENTS : 8 SERVINGS

6 chauve-souris (flying-fox bats)

$1/2$ lb onions, chopped

2 shallots

2 cloves garlic, minced (optional)

$1/2$ lb very ripe pommes d'amour or tomatoes

1 bouquet of thyme and parsley

whole peppercorns and salt to taste

1 bottle dry red wine, preferably from burgundy

1 cup oil, preferably $1/2$ olive oil and $1/2$ sunflower oil

$1/2$ cup crème fraîche or heavy cream

Fried or grilled croutons

Prepare the chauve-souris. Discard wings, skin, and head. Remove interior organs and guts. Wash well with vinegared water and cut into pieces. Place in a bowl to marinate with half of the onions, the shallots, garlic, thyme, parsley, peppercorns, salt and wine. Chill for at least 12 hours.

When ready to cook, remove the pieces of meat and reserve the marinade. Heat the oil, add the rest of the onions and sauté lightly. Add the meat and cook, turning the pieces over, until well browned. Stir in the pommes d'amour cut in quarters, and the reserved marinade. Cover and simmer for one hour. Stir occasionally to prevent sticking.

Before serving, discard any small bones saving the meat, and thicken the sauce with crème fraîche. Adjust seasonings, transfer to a serving platter and surround with croutons.

**HERVÉ KOENIG**

### THE CHAUVE-SOURIS (FLYING-FOX BAT)

*Mauritius, isolated for centuries from the rest of the world, was an ideal habitat for a variety of unique, rare, and unusual fauna – the dodo bird being the most famous, and the mammalian flying-fox bat probably the least known. This species of bat, which thrived in parts of Asia and on some islands of the Pacific Ocean, was probably introduced from the Orient early on in its civilization. The Chinese people had for a very long time ranked it high on their list of gastronomic delicacies.*

*These austere creatures, resting by day in the protective shadows of the woods, spread their six foot parachute wings at dusk and lazily started on their nocturnal foray. At the forest edge hunters would gather to watch the flock of bats take flight and aim their guns in the twilight. One had to be an excellent shot to bring one down, and retrieving the prize was even harder in the dark. Mauritians, like the Chinese, relished the bat for its ambrosial meat – this creature after all gorged itself with fruit, particularly the fruit of palm trees. Cyclones and bullets took their toll and when it became evident that the survival of the flying-fox bat was threatened, conservation measures were taken and hunting was outlawed. Even so...*

# DESSERTS

# Sorbet of fresh litchis or passion fruit

### Ingredients

3 lbs fresh litchis, excluding stems and leaves (about 75 fruits)

1/2 lb sugar

3 cups water

Peel the litchis and discard the pits. Crush the pulp in a food processor and strain, or pass through a food mill. Stir the sugar in the water until completely dissolved and add to the juice. Place to freeze in a hand-cranked or electric ice cream maker, or in the freezer.

We have excluded those sorbets made with fruits which also grow in Europe such as strawberries and raspberries. Omitted also are the pearly white and frosty pink jamalaques (Eugenia Malaccencis) so attractive to the eye, but insipid to the palate. Hog plums (fruits de Cythere) could surely be used to make a most original sorbet. But as for bananas which find favour in other countries in both sorbets and ice creams, Mauritians prefer to enjoy them at the breakfast table or cooked according to their lore.

# Island fantasy

## Ingredients : 4 servings

2 ripe coconuts, split in half — shells included

8 scoops coconut ice cream

$^3/_4$ cup pineapple juice

$^1/_3$ cup coconut punch

$^1/_3$ cup old rum

1 ripe banana

The coconut halves will be used as serving dishes. Place them in the freezer two hours before serving to frost them.

Place the sliced banana, the pineapple juice, and the coconut punch in a blender and mix until homogenized. Add in the old rum and two or three ice cubes. Blend for one to two minutes.

Arrange the coconut ice cream in the coconut halves and nap with the fruit and rum mixture.

Lovers of coconut are encouraged to nibble on the serving dish while enjoying the dessert!

**Jacqueline Dalais**

# COCONUT MACAROONS

### INGREDIENTS

1 ripe coconut – approx. $^3/_4$ lb of coconut meat

1 cup sugar

1 egg, separated

$^1/_2$ vanilla bean or $^1/_2$ teaspoon vanilla powder

2 tablespoons flour

1 teaspoon butter or margarine

Peel and grate the coconut. Mix with the sugar, egg yolk, vanilla, flour, and butter or margarine. Fold in the stiffly beaten egg white just prior to baking. Drop batter, by tablespoonfuls, on a buttered baking sheet and bake in medium oven for about 20 minutes. Adjust baking time so macaroons are soft or crunchy – depending on taste.

# SWEET POTATO PUDDING WITH CHOCOLATE AND COCONUT

### INGREDIENTS : 5 TO 6 SERVINGS

2 lbs sweet potatoes (patates douces)

$^1/_2$ lb coconut, peeled and finely grated

$^1/_4$ lb bittersweet cooking chocolate, melted 300 grams of sugar

3 eggs

1 vanilla bean or 1 teaspoon vanilla powder

1 tablespoon rum

Caramel to line pudding mould

Boil the sweet potatoes until very tender. Peel them while they are still hot (discarding any fibres present), and purée in a mixer. Stir the sugar into the melted chocolate and add to the purée sweet potatoes with the whole eggs, vanilla and rum. Beat well until mixture is homogeneous. Transfer to a caramel-lined mould and cook au bain marie (in a bath of hot water) for 50 to 60 minutes. Serve cold accompanied, if desired, by a light vanilla custard.

*NOTE :* *Patates douces, (sweet potatoes of the Malaga pink variety with purplish skins and white flesh), make a wonderful merger with chocolate in purées, candies, cakes etc ...*

# CANDIED PAPAYA
# (PAPAYE CRISTALLISEE - OU TAPÉE!)

Follow directions for papaya compote (as below) and at the end keep the compote on low heat until all the syrup is absorbed. Place to dry in the sun for a whole day (protect from bees and flies with netting). Sprinkle with vanilla sugar and store in securely sealed jars to protect from humidity.

**HERVÉ KOENIG**

CANDIED FRUITS : THE CONFECTION OF CANDIED FRUITS IS VERY POPULAR IN MAURITIUS. TWO FRUITS ARE MORE COMMONLY USED: THE PAMPLEMOUSSES (WHICH IS NOT THE EUROPEAN GRAPE FRUIT) AND THE PAPAYA.

# CANDIED PAMPLEMOUSSE

The pamplemousse which grows in Mauritius hails from the pummelo family. It is a large fruit with very thick and bitter skin. The flesh is pink, not as juicy as the grapefruit, but very pleasant to eat when marinated in sugar.

### INGREDIENTS

3 pamplemousses

7 lbs sugar

3 litres water

Quarter the pamplemousses. Remove the flesh and reserve the skins. Grate the skins lightly to remove the zest and place the white skins to soak in lightly salted water for about 24 hours, changing the water 3 to 4 times. Then, drain and press the skins to remove as much water as possible. Blanch them twice in boiling water - for 15 minutes each time. Rinse under cold water, drain, and press dry. Place in the sun for about $1/2$ hour. Meanwhile prepare a syrup with 6 lbs of sugar and the water. Boil the syrup until it becomes thick and forms a thread between the fingers. Place the skins in the syrup and let cook until total absorption of the syrup. Remove from heat, cool a little, then dip in sugar so that they are completely coated. Place to dry in hot sunlight and store in a tightly covered jar.

# BANANA BONBONS WITH ORANGE PEEL

### INGREDIENTS

10 very ripe bananas

sugar: use half the weight of the peeled bananas

$1/2$ vanilla bean or $1/2$ teaspoon vanilla powder or extract

1 teaspoon grated orange or lemon rind

2 inches orange or lemon rind, cut into fine juliennes

Mash the bananas with a fork or in a blender. Beat in the sugar, vanilla, and the grated and julienned orange or lemon rind. Cook over low heat, stirring, for 10 minutes. Remove from heat and cool until mixture is warm.

Shape into little balls and coat with sugar.

# SAFFRON

THERE ARE TWO TYPES, AND THEY ARE TOTALLY UNRELATED. ONE IS THE SAFFRON OF THE INDIES, KNOWN AS TURMERIC OR CURCUMA, WHOSE YELLOW RHIZOME IS USED IN CURRIES. THE OTHER, CALLED ORIENTAL OR SPANISH SAFFRON (CROCUS SAFRANIS) IS THE DRIED STAMEN OF THE CULTIVATED CROCUS PLANT, ORIGINATING IN THE EAST AND BROUGHT TO SPAIN BY THE ARABS.

THE SAFFRON OF THE INDIES CAN BE USED EITHER FRESH, OR DRIED AND CRUSHED INTO A FINE POWDER. THE FRESH RHIZOME HAS A BITTER TASTE AND A GINGER-LIKE FLAVOUR. CRUSHED INTO A PULP, IT GIVES CURRIES AND ACHARDS A UNIQUE AND DELICATE FLAVOUR - IT IS THE **SAFFRAN VERT** OF MAURITIUS.

SPANISH SAFFRON IS CULTIVATED MAINLY IN SPAIN, BUT ALSO IN SOME PARTS OF FRANCE AND CENTRAL EUROPE. IT IS THE MOST EXPENSIVE OF SPICES - IN OLDER TIMES WHEN THE VALUE OF THE RUPEE EQUALLED ITS WEIGHT OF SILVER, THE PRICE OF SAFFRON WAS SIMILARLY BASED. FORTUNATELY, THANKS TO ITS CONCENTRATED STRENGTH, IT CAN BE USED VERY PARSIMONIOUSLY: A SMALL AMOUNT SUFFICES FOR MOST DISHES. SPANISH SAFFRON CAN BE BOUGHT IN FILAMENTS OR POWDER FORM AND ITS PERFUMED FLAVOUR IS RELEASED WHEN DISSOLVED. IT IS RECOMMENDED TO USE OTHER SPICES LIGHTLY IN THOSE DISHES WHERE SAFFRON PLAYS A MAJOR ROLE - TO NAME A FEW: PAELLA, BOUILLABAISSE, AND BRIANI.

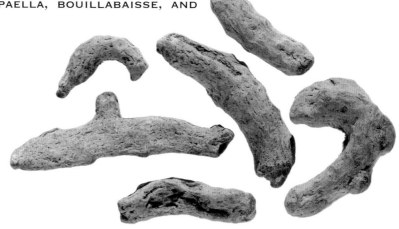

# CHUTNEYS, ACHARDS, SAUCES

# OCTOPUS CHUTNEY

## INGREDIENTS : 6 TO 8 SERVINGS

1 lb dried octopus

1 medium onion

2 teaspoons vinegar or lemon juice

2 tablespoons olive oil

Chillies, garlic, ginger root and parsley

Choose baby octopuses which have been properly cleaned and left to dry in plenty of sun and wind. They can be dried in the kitchen, providing one can tolerate the odour! Place the separated tentacles to grill over a charcoal fire, then pound in a mortar. Separate the meat from the little suction cups and discard any scorched surfaces.

Cut meat into very fine slices and mix in the rest of the ingredients according to taste.

## NOTE :

*Fresh octopus may be substituted for the dried specimen, although the dish will be more like a salad than a chutney. Fresh octopus must first be boiled, and the tentacles scraped and cleaned thoroughly before using.*

---

**CHUTNEYS (CHATINI) :** OF INDIAN ORIGIN, CHUTNEYS ARE CONDIMENTS MADE FROM ONE TO TWO PRIMARY INGREDIENTS SEASONED WITH GARLIC, GINGER, CHILLIES, SALT, AND PEPPER - AND TO WHICH IS ADDED A LITTLE VINEGAR AND SOMETIMES SOME OIL. (SEE RECIPES). CHUTNEYS ARE SERVED WITH RICE.

---

# CHUTNEY OF DRIED SALTED FISH

## INGREDIENTS : 6 SERVINGS

$^1/_3$ lb (5 oz) dry salted fish.

1 small onion, thinly sliced or minced

dash of crushed chilli and garlic (optional)

1 teaspoon oil (use 2 teaspoons for white salted fish)

1 tablespoon lemon juice or vinegar

1 branch each of thyme and parsley

Pepper

Desalt the fish by soaking in cold water for about one hour. Drain and pat dry. Fry until crisp, or if you prefer grill the fish. Crumble into small pieces and mix in the onion, chilli and garlic. Stir in the oil and lemon juice, and sprinkle with thyme, chopped parsley, and freshly ground pepper.

## NOTE :

*The "Snoek", sold by weight or in pieces, is most commonly used. If you prefer the "white" variety of salted fish, use ¹/₂ lb.*

# GREEN MANGO CHUTNEY

## INGREDIENTS : 6 TO 8 SERVINGS

2 lbs "green" or unripe mangoes

3 tablespoons oil

1 small onion, finely chopped

1 teaspoon crushed ginger

1 teaspoon crushed garlic

1 teaspoon turmeric

1 teaspoon crushed chillies

1 tablespoon vinegar

Salt

Peel the mangoes, then grate them using the coarsest side of the grater. As an alternative the mangoes may be cut into chunks and grated in the food processor.

In a skillet heat the oil, then add in the onion, ginger, garlic, turmeric and chillies. Cook over gentle heat, stirring for about two minutes. Remove from heat and stir in the vinegar. Add the grated mango, mix well and season with salt.

POMME D'AMOUR: MUST NOT BE CONFUSED WITH THE FRUIT OF THE GARDEN OF EDEN PRESENTED TO ADAM! THIS SMALL TOMATO BEARS THE SAME APPELLATION IN SOME PARTS OF SOUTHERN FRANCE. IT IS BLESSED WITH AMAZING FLAVOUR AND IS ALSO USED TO MAKE DELICIOUS JAMS AND CONFECTIONS. IT BECAME AN INTEGRAL PART OF MANY OF OUR RECIPES - IN FACT, A USURPER IN MANY RECIPES WHERE IT DID NOT ORIGINALLY BELONG - AS IN CURRIES. IN THE WORLD OF MAURITIAN CHUTNEYS, THE CHATINI DE POMME D'AMOUR REIGNS SUPREME AND HAS NO EQUAL!

# VEGETABLE ACHARDS

*A type of pickle of Indian origin, typically served as a dish to accompany meals with rice. Exotic and savoury, achards can in fact complement almost any dish. Dried powdered turmeric may also be used with excellent results instead of saffran vert if not available.*

## INGREDIENTS

1 lb cauliflower
1 lb carrots
1 lb cabbage
1 lb string beans
1/2 lb pearl onions
1/2 lb fresh turmeric (or 2 tablespoons turmeric powder)
8 large cloves garlic
10 long chillies
4 tablespoons vinegar
1 teaspoon whole peppercorns
2 tablespoons crushed ginger root
1 cup olive oil mixed with 1 or 2 teaspoons mustard

*ACHARDS DE BILIMBIS*

Separate the cauliflower into small flowerets, discarding the tough stems. Scrape the carrots and cut into sticks 2 to 3 inches x 1/2 inch. Shred the cabbage as for a salad. If the beans are not stringless (mange-tout), remove strings by snapping tip and pulling down on one side and then the other. Slice in two lenghtwise and then cut in half. Peel onions and cut two in thin slices.

Place the vegetables on a tray (or any flat surface)laying them on top of a cloth. Place them for a whole day in the hot sun.

Crush the turmeric, ginger root and garlic together. In a large saucepan, heat 1/4 cup oil, add the mixture and cook, stirring, for 1 or 2 minutes. Add the sliced onion and chillies, and cook for one more minute. Add the remainder of the oil and when it comes to a light boil, add all the vegetables at once. Stir and cook for 3 to 4 minutes over medium heat – the less they are cooked, the crunchier they will be. Remove and let cool. Place into jars and cover tightly.

Achards will keep a long time when refrigerated and kept tightly covered in a jar flooded with oil.

**ACHARDS** (ACHAR - ACHAAR): PREPARATION WITH A BASE OF OIL, VINEGAR, SPICES, AND FRESH TURMERIC. IT CONVENIENTLY PRESERVES VEGETABLES, HEART OF PALM AND LIMES. OF INDIAN ORIGIN, AND SIMILAR TO THE "VINDAYE", IT IS SERVED WITH RICE.

# Sauce papa

*A venerable island condiment with a base of lemon juice and a twist of red hot charcoal...*

## Ingredients

6 juicy lemons
3 cloves garlic
1 small piece fresh ginger root
1 small onion
1 tablespoon (15 grams) very hot chilli
(more or less as desired)
Salt

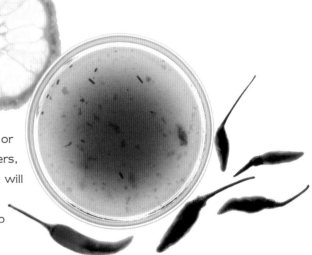

Squeeze the lemons. Crush the garlic, ginger, onion
and chilli to a paste and add to the lemon juice. Take one or
two pieces of red hot charcoal, shake to remove the cinders,
and plunge into the sauce for a few seconds. The sauce will
sizzle when exposed to this devilish shock treatment - and
prove to be a heavenly condiment for those among us who
are not faint of heart!

This sauce is particularly stimulating with fried foods, such as fish, vegetable fritters etc.

# Sauce "ti malice"

## Ingredients
1/2 lb shallots
3 to 4 baby onions
Parsley sprigs
5 tablespoons (75 gms) crushed hot chilli
2 tablespoons oil
2 cups lemon juice (or "Bigarade juice")
Sprig of thyme
Salt, pepper

Chop the shallots, onions and parsley. Mix well
with the chilli and oil. Stir in the lemon juice.
Season with thyme, salt, and freshly ground
pepper.

This sauce accompanies fried or grilled fish, and
chicken.

# INDEX OF RECIPES

# MEATS, POULTRY, VENISON

# DESSERTS

# CHUTNEYS, SAUCES

Our sincere thanks to the chefs :

FIROZ **ABDOOL**
RÉMY **COTTE**
RICHARD **FREDERIC**
RICARDO **KISNASAMY**
RAJ **LUCKHUN**
BERTY **MERIZA**
FRANCIS **PATHÉ**
VEEREN **PILLAY**
GÉRARD **PYANEENANDEE**
SÉBASTIEN **STEPHEN**
BAGEEROW **SUKHOO**

who have mixed their boundless talent with infinite passion
in the preparation of the recipes in the kitchens
kindly put at our disposal by the **BEACHCOMBER GROUP** hotels.

And our deepest gratitude goes to the "chef" graphic designer
**PASCAL LAGESSE** who has generously added his fragrant
flavours to the layout of the book.

We would like to welcome a few new contributors to
this new edition and to thank **VALERIE MAYER**
for having translated a few texts.